ACTIVATING THE GIFT OF PROPHECY

OTHER BOOKS BY
JERMAINE AND REBECCA FRANCIS

Break Up with Defeat by Jermaine Francis

Thx! The Secret to Being Grateful by Rebecca Francis

ACTIVATING THE GIFT OF PROPHECY

YOUR GUIDE TO RECEIVING &
SHARING WHAT GOD IS SAYING

JERMAINE & REBECCA FRANCIS

DESTINY IMAGE® PUBLISHERS, INC.
P.O. Box 310, Shippensburg, PA 17257-0310
"Promoting Inspired Lives."

This book and all other Destiny Image and Destiny Image Fiction books are available at Christian bookstores and distributors worldwide.

Cover design by Eileen Rockwell
Interior design by Terry Clifton

For more information on foreign distributors, call 717-532-3040.
Reach us on the Internet: www.destinyimage.com.

ISBN 13 TP: 978-0-7684-5150-4
ISBN 13 eBook: 978-0-7684-5151-1
ISBN 13 HC: 978-0-7684-5153-5
ISBN 13 LP: 978-0-7684-5152-8

For Worldwide Distribution, Printed in the U.S.A.
2 3 4 5 6 7 8 / 23 22 21 20

CONTENTS

FOREWORD

by *Apostles Tom and Jane Hamon*

Each believer is given continuous revelation by the
Holy Spirit to benefit not just himself but all.
—1 CORINTHIANS 12:7 The Passion Translation

The following are just a few testimonies we have received through the years about how God's prophetic voice through us has impacted people's lives:

> When you two prophesied to me last year, God completely healed me of epilepsy.

> Your prophetic words spoke about how God was going to open my barren womb and bless me with many children, and now I am pregnant with my fifth child!

> You guys prophesied to me that God was going to bless me as a writer, and now I am working on my fifth book!

> The prophetic words you released helped me embrace my calling to ministry, and now I travel and speak all around the world.

1

During the past 40 years of ministry together, it has been amazing for us to see how one word from God can change everything! As a matter of fact, we believe releasing the voice of God is one of the most powerful tools we can use to unlock destiny and freedom, bring healing and deliverance, impart spiritual gifts for breakthrough, and advance the Kingdom of God.

When we were in our early 20s, we began to walk out the call of God together. We worked with Tom's father, Bishop Bill Hamon, in the offices of Christian International and even pioneered and pastored our first little church in the Arizona desert. The ministry eventually moved to Florida where we set up our headquarters and began to hold regular training conferences to teach, train, and activate people to hear the voice of God. We also pioneered Christian International Family Church (now Vision Church) during this time to help establish our base.

In the early days, Bishop Hamon did all the work—all the preaching, praying, and prophesying. We would stand with him while he ministered to hundreds of people and hold the microphone and pray, and we would occasionally get a little word to share. But during one conference, he became extremely sick with walking pneumonia and realized he couldn't do it all himself.

That morning, he told us he would not be the one prophesying to the people, and that he was going to divide the staff into teams who would minister to those attending the conference. We were horrified! We said, "Bishop, they aren't coming to hear from us, they are coming to hear from you!"

"No!" he replied. "They are coming to hear from God—and you are trained and equipped. Now you will be the ones to minister to them."

Yikes!

Needless to say, we all fasted lunch that day and read as much of the Bible as we possibly could in that hour, praying in tongues frantically and begging God to use us. To say we were nervous would be an understatement. But when the time came, Bishop was right. We had been trained to hear God's voice and we were equipped to minister the word of the Lord to our assigned teams of people.

By God's grace, we did it! Whew! We realized that Bishop Hamon had set an example for us by his demonstration and empowered us through activation so that when the time came, we could step into the full impartation to fulfill our calling. We have been prophesying ever since! Bishop Hamon reproduced himself in us, teaching us everything he knew, laying hands on us for the anointing, and then pushed us out to do it!

Since that time, Christian International has trained hundreds of thousands of people worldwide to hear God's voice and minister to others so they can change their world. We have many, many methods of activations that are taught through our Apostolic Prophetic Training Modules, which involve not just the activation of the gifts but also the shaping of a person's character. Bishop Hamon has taught that God is more interested in making a mighty person rather than a mighty ministry.

We also have a full-time, on-campus Bible College of students who don't just receive a Bible education, but also a spiritual activation of the gifts of the Holy Spirit. Our students all serve on our local church prophetic teams and become very proficient in hearing and releasing God's voice.

More than 15 years ago, two students came to our Bible College, fell in love, were married, and began their own journey of walking out the call of God on their lives together.

Jermaine and Rebecca Francis answered the call to be taught, trained, equipped, and activated to hear God's voice and minister to others. Just as Bishop Hamon laid hands on us, so also we all laid hands on them and released an impartation. Now, not only have they each prophesied to thousands of people all around the world with great anointing and power, they also carry the mantle and the mandate to raise up their generation to do the same.

Today Jermaine and Rebecca are considered prophets to nations, authors, speakers, and gifted leaders in the body of Christ. The anointing that has been upon Bishop Hamon and our lives has now been imparted to them and they are running with it. We represent three generations running together to, in Bishop's words, "Reproduce reproducers who reproduce reproducers."

Activating the Gift of Prophecy is a clarion call to the arising prophetic generation to draw on all of what the previous generations have pioneered—and build into the future. Let God activate your prophetic gift so you too can hear God's voice and change your world.

Apostles Tom and Jane Hamon
Senior Leaders
Vision Church @ Christian International

PREFACE

Hearing God is at the foundation of Christianity. That's right. You heard God when you got saved! Salvation wasn't the end, though. There's so much more to hearing and responding to God's voice.

When you hear God on an ongoing basis, throughout each day, for yourself, your responsibilities, your environment, and the people around you, you will start fully demonstrating the Kingdom of God.

Demonstrating God's Kingdom cannot be done apart from hearing and obeying His voice. Dr. Tim Hamon, in his book *Upon This Rock*, proves this best: "Jesus was born to be a king. His purpose as a king is to 'bear witness to the truth.' A kingdom is where a king's word is law. Jesus is saying His kingdom is not a geographical or political place such as Rome; rather His Kingdom is wherever someone hears His voice."[1]

In short, the Kingdom of God is everywhere His voice is heard and obeyed. So how can you be in the Kingdom except that you hear His voice?

Is This for Me, Right Now?

Is God calling you to function in prophetic ministry? Well, you're reading this book, so we would say yes. God often leads us by first putting a desire in our hearts. If you have any interest in it, then you're probably called to it.

Let us be the first to welcome you to the club. We have been waiting for you. This book will help get you started on your journey. We promise you if read this book, you will be prophesying before you finish it. It's time for you to do the stuff and not just watch others do it. Every believer has a part to play in what God is doing on earth today.

God has a way of leading our lives and calling each one of us to walk in the destiny that He has for us. He knows the way we should go, and He leads us to the right path. We each have different paths that lead us to the prophetic calling on our lives. You also have your own personal and unique journey with God.

Jermaine's Journey into Prophetic Ministry

I felt a call from the Lord into full-time ministry when I was about 17 years old. I received several prophetic words during this time. There was a lady who sat a few rows behind my mom and I at church. Every Sunday she would say, "You know you're called to be a prophet, right?" I would smile and say, "Thank you." I believed her; I just wasn't sure what that meant at the time.

Random people would have dreams about me ministering to large groups of people. This was all in a short, about six-month, period of time. The most notable prophetic word came one night at youth club. I was a youth leader, and it was the beginning of my senior year of high school. It was a Tuesday night, midweek service. We had a guest minister that night and he offered an altar call for something I don't even remember. While I was at the altar praying for people, a tall guy I had never seen before, or since, came over and put his arms around me. He held me in a tight hug, then he started to prophesy to me about my future.

The word was all about a call on my life to be a prophet to the nations and bring the word of the Lord to many people. I fell on the ground weeping from a deep place inside me. God revealed to me purpose, destiny, calling, identity, love. It affected me in a significant way. I got up from that moment and began to pursue God for the call that He had on my life. That pursuit led me to Valor Christian College, formally World Harvest Bible College. Then it led me to Christian International where they train and equip people in the prophetic.

For more than 50 years, Christian International (CI) has been teaching people about the prophetic. My wife, Rebecca, and I now work on staff at CI. We also travel nationally and internationally teaching and training on the prophetic. We have personally prophesied to more than 10,000 people. I am now doing what the prophetic word I received at 17 years old said I would be doing.

Christian International Ministries was founded by Bishop Bill Hamon. He is considered the father of the modern-day prophetic movement. He started training and teaching the prophetic when no one thought it was still a valid ministry. For more than 60 years he has helped to restore biblical understanding of prophetic ministry. Terms like prophet and prophetic were made accessible by him.

Rebecca's Journey into Prophetic Ministry

When I was 14 years old, my church hosted a prophetic conference—by accident! A church nearly two hours away had scheduled this particular conference long in advance. Their guest speaker was Gale Sheehan, a traveling prophet from Christian International. When it was time for the conference, the original location had a problem with their building—the ceiling collapsed! The venue was unusable. So, the pastor began contacting churches nearby looking for a building to use.

a male

He finally found our church, two hours away, which was the only church willing and available for that event, on those dates, on short notice. Ours was a small church, and my large family of eight was part of almost every team. I was on the worship team—a hilarious story for another time. My siblings served in childcare; my mom cleaned the church; my dad worked the sound equipment. So when this conference came to our church, we instantly became part of the event "staff."

One by one, over three days, each person in my family received a personal prophecy from Gale Sheehan. And each one of us wept and were transformed by the word. We'd experienced God's voice before, but never anything like that. Usually when someone prophesied, it was either built up with intense tongues and shaking, or it was prepared over days, weeks, or months, like a slow puzzle God was building with the person. We'd never seen someone prophesy at will to everyone in the room, not to mention the prophetic word being accurate and profoundly impactful to each person.

I didn't receive a prophecy until the end of the event. I had been in childcare during all the services, so at the end of the last service, my mom approached Gale and asked him to prophesy to me. I had seen my whole family fall into puddles of tears or their faces stunned with shock at what was said to them. So I expected that too. I didn't cry during the prophecy, though. I just thought about it. My face was straight and my eyes were fixed ahead. No expression, barely even bowing my head. If I had been the one prophesying, I'd have thought this girl isn't getting anything out of this. But I didn't know what to expect, so that's how I reacted.

The following week I typed the entire prophecy—it was five pages. I liked it. I liked what kind of person it made me sound like. I wanted to grow up to be the person the prophecy said I'd be.

Today, 20 years later, I am still fulfilling that word. Of every prophecy I've received since, that one was the most overarching, covering what seems to be my entire life. That prophecy matches my life perfectly.

The coolest part of the story is what happened when I was 21, just seven years later. I felt called to attend CI's Bible college, so I moved to Santa Rosa Beach, Florida, and got a job in retail in September 2005. In early December, the dean of the Bible college approached me about a job opening within CI as an administrative assistant. I'd have a desk, and I'd file and create Excel reports, stuff like that. I thought a desk was better than folding and refolding shirts all day, so I took the job. What I didn't realize at the time was that my boss would be Gale Sheehan. The very person who gave me my first prophetic word.

That word became a road map to my life and now the person God used to release the word to me is part of helping me fulfill that prophetic word. Gale Sheehan gave me my first speaking opportunity on a ministry trip. He hired me for my first graphic design job, which I now use in my self-publishing business. Every step of the way he has helped unlock abilities in me that I didn't know I had and that serve my destiny. It's amazing how the prophetic word opens the way for it to be fulfilled.

That first prophetic word is the foundation for what God has been building in my life over the past two decades. The prophetic word is priceless to me, and I believe it will be to all those who receive it!

Why This Book

A few years ago, Jermaine was helping at a book table for one of the Christian International leaders at an event. Someone came up the table asking what the books were about. After an explanation, the person said, "Wow, that's a lot of good content, but I'm new to all this. Which one of the books will help me start prophesying to people?" Jermaine stopped for a moment and looked at the books. None of the books would do that.

I said, "Sorry, we don't have a book like that currently." I did recommend that he come to our on-site prophetic training program. Twice a year, every January and September in Santa Rosa Beach, Florida, we offer hands-on prophetic training. More than 300,000 around the world have gone through that training and are now prophesying.

This experience at the book table started the desire in us to write a book that someone can pick up, read, and then be activated to start prophesying and ministering the heart of God to others. What you now hold in your hand is that book.

In 2018 we were at a gathering of prophets from all around the world. Some of them were household names among Charismatics. Others we had never heard of but were excited to meet. It's a bit intense to be in an event full of prophets! Even though we were all prophets, we quickly realized not everyone perceives prophets and prophecy the same way. We each come from different prophetic backgrounds.

On the first night, Rebecca was asked by the overseeing prophet to come to the platform and select someone to prophecy over. This is what we do with our lives, so it was a simple request. Rebecca prophesied for about five minutes over a younger girl sitting in the back row. At different times in the word, I could hear people reacting all over the room.

That part was surprising because everyone in the room was a prophet. It was like a convention for people who label themselves as hearing God. So to see other prophets surprised at the way someone in the room heard God was itself, well, surprising.

The next day, one of the prophets asked us how we did what we did. He explained that he has prophesied countless times and is comfortable knowing when God is speaking to him. But he said he would not know how to randomly select a person and speak on behalf of God for five minutes with such depth. He even asked if there was a book we had written or read explaining how to do it.

The short answer to this prophet's question was that we had trained to do that by doing prophetic exercises we call "activations." That conversation confirmed the need for this book that Jermaine had already felt for years. This same book you now are reading.

You Have a Part to Play

You may or may not consider yourself a prophetic person—but you are. Whether you have been prophesying for years or have never prophesied before, by the end of this book you will be. The insights and truths in this book will unlock the gift of prophecy from the Holy Spirit in you. No matter your background or what you have previously been taught, you are called by God to hear His voice and impact the world.

You're not reading this book by accident. You're reading it by divine appointment. There is a move of God coming to the earth and we need you to be fully equipped to take your place in it. This is your time to be activated in prophetic ministry.

ENDNOTE

1. Tim Hamon, *Upon This Rock: The Kingdom of God, the Voice of God, and the Third Reformation* (Santa Rosa Beach, FL: Christian International Publishing, 2017), 24.

INTRODUCTION

by *Bill Hamon*

Jermaine and Rebecca have done an excellent job in presenting the wisdom needed for properly ministering the prophetic ministry to people. They attended Christian International's Ministry Training College for several years. They were thoroughly trained in the principles, protocols, and proper practices for ministering personal prophecy to others. They taught and trained many saints in the United States and several other nations. For example, they traveled to Korea and taught and trained people the prophetic ministry using Christian International's manual for teaching the prophetic entitled, the *Manual for Ministering Spiritual Gifts*. They prophesied to more than 400 individuals during that week of teaching, activating, and prophesying.

In 1985 I wrote the *Manual for Ministering Spiritual Gifts*. In the late 1970s and early 1980s, I would travel to churches teaching and activating church members in the prophetic, which is activating saints in the gifts of the Holy Spirit. But most times when I would return to that church six months later, they had not maintained or advanced in the prophetic ministry. After discussing this with several pastors, I discovered the problem. The pastors revealed that they did not have the revelation, knowledge, or experience to teach, train, and activate saints in prophetic ministry. They needed a teaching manual to help them. So, I wrote the 300-page teaching manual with teaching outlines, scriptural instructions, and activations. Now, more than 300,000 saints and ministers have been trained in the *Manual for Ministering Spiritual Gifts* in most the nations.

In 1973, God gave me the divine visitation that gave revelation and divine enablement to minister in personal prophecy to numerous people in one service. One major prophet prophesied that God was giving me the anointing "to be a reproducer of reproducers who would also reproduce reproducers, who could train and equip people in prophetic ministry." To fulfill that prophetic word, we began Schools of the Holy Spirit and later Prophetic Seminars. I wrote the manual for the reproducers to teach, train, and equip others to be able to do the same.

To make sure the church understood prophets and the ministry of personal prophecy, I wrote *Prophets and Personal Prophecy,* which was published in 1986. After the Prophetic Movement was birthed in October 1988, I wrote *Prophets and the Prophetic Movement.* This book covers the ministry of the prophets, what the Prophetic Movement restored in the church, and guidelines for proper ways to minister in personal prophecy.

There became a need for much more clarity and understanding concerning giving, receiving, and fulfilling personal prophecy. So, next I wrote *Prophets—Pitfalls to Avoid and Principles to Practice.* These books have become the major resources to help prophetic people to ministepersonal prophecy with wisdom, accuracy, and balance.

Prophets, Jermaine and Rebecca have been taught these books and now they have taught them numerous times to others along with the manual. They have pulled together the knowledge, wisdom, and experience they gained over the years and have written this book to introduce new beginners to prophetic ministry and to help mature those who have already been introduced to prophetic ministry.

Bless you Jermaine and Rebecca, know that you are a fulfillment of prophecy that was spoken to me, that I would have the anointing to be a reproducer who would reproduce reproducers. In the 1980s, I reproduced the prophetic ministry in my children and their generation, they then reproduced others in the 1990s, and they reproduced you in the first decade of the 21st Century.

Now in the second decade and continuing, you are reproducing others with the same anointing, wisdom, and grace. This book will be an additional extension of your reproducing ministry as my many books have been for my ministry. You have made your Bishop PaPa proud to see you faithfully fulfilling your calling from God to co-labor with Christ in building His Church.

BILL HAMON
Bishop of Christian International Apostolic-Global Network
Author of *The Eternal Church; Prophets and Personal Prophecy; Prophets and the Prophetic Movement; Prophets, Pitfalls, and Principles; Apostles, Prophets, and the Coming Moves of God; The Day of the Saints; Who Am I & Why Am I Here; Prophetic Scriptures Yet to Be Fulfilled—During the 3rd and Final Reformation; Seventy Reasons for Speaking in Tongues, How Can These Things Be?* and *God's World War III*

Chapter 1

YOU CAN PROPHESY

You can prophesy. You can hear God and can communicate what He reveals to you. For most believers, this truth has been way overcomplicated. It's simple. We were created to hear God and to be prophetic people, even if you are not called to be a prophet. Hearing God is the foundation for building the Church and for a thriving relationship with Him. Jesus says in John 10:27: *"My sheep hear my voice, and I know them, and they follow me."* We talk more about this later, as well as the fact that we're even commanded to desire to prophesy. Imagine that!

So, are you ready to grow in the prophetic gifting? It's exciting! Congratulations on taking this journey, and thanks for taking it with us.

Jermaine's First Time Prophesying

When I was about 18 years old and attending Bible college, one of my class instructors had been connected to Christian International and had completed their prophetic training. One day he said, "We're going to do a prophetic activation." I thought, *What's that? Sounds painful and weird.* He told everyone to partner with someone else in the room. So, I tried to find someone in the room who looked as scared as I did, or more. I saw a classmate who looked nervous too.

Then he said for us to take our partner's hand and close our eyes. "We're going to pray and ask God to show us something for the person whose hand we are holding," he said. I thought, *That's weird, but ok.* I didn't think I was going to get anything, that it would work for everyone else but not me.

19

(handwritten margin note: Step 2)

We prayed and I immediately felt like my partner needed a job. The instructor then told us to pray with that person according to what we received from the Lord. I prayed for her about finding the right job, with a proper pay and schedule. Then I asked her if that was correct. She looked up at me in tears and said that's exactly what she needed and was praying about that morning. It was a direct confirmation for her. I was shocked. I couldn't believe I got a sensing from the Lord that ministered to someone else. I felt empowered, but still nervous.

God wants to use you the same way, because you were created for it.

Prophecy has Become Overcomplicated

(handwritten margin note: a "given")

Hearing God in our current culture has become a weird thing. Either you're crazy and should be locked up in the loony bin, or it's some elite spiritual level someone else has reached. Well, guess what, it's neither. Hearing God is the right of every born-again believer. Hearing God should be part of our daily life. Jesus says as a general fact that we, His sheep, hear His voice and He knows us and we follow Him (John 10:27). There was no hype around it. Just a matter of fact letting you know how this prophecy thing works—you are My sheep; you hear My voice. That's it.

(handwritten margin note: do not give in to impedence)

The enemy and the flesh want to make prophesying hard and confusing. Jesus wants to make it simple for us. It's been the enemy's strategy to cloud and hide the truth about a believer's right to hear God. He is trying to create distance between God and us. The Holy Spirit is passionately coming after us, to connect us to God. Like the song "Reckless Love" by Cory Asbury says: "There's no wall You won't kick down, lie You won't tear down, coming after me." God is removing anything that distances us from Him.

Hearing Is Access

It's normal to hear the voice of God. We were created for it. Proverbs 20:12 says, *"The hearing ear and the seeing eye, the Lord has made them both."* Every part of our created nature is designed to hear God. We can look at Genesis and see God's first interaction with man. God walked with Adam and spoke with him. Adam had a relationship with God; there was intimacy and closeness. In any kind and healthy relationship, communication is critical. God and Adam had that.

God's desire to connect with humankind has not changed since Genesis. God wants to talk to us not to share information, but to share hearts. Him sharing His heart with us and us with Him. That intent has not changed. It became harder for humans to connect to God after Adam activated our sin nature. A wall was put between us and God. It did not stop His desire, it only prevented access. God still desires to talk to us, to all His children.

Even when sin was in the way, God found a way to still talk to His people. He used prophets in the Old Testament to talk to them. He gave instructions and directions through prophetic voices. He raised up prophets during each part of Israel's history, to share His heart with them. He never left them without His voice speaking to them somehow.

When Jesus came, He became the Wi-Fi signal that reconnected us to God. He busted open the doors of communication and connection between God and humankind again. We no longer need a prophet to be our go-between to God. Each one of us can access Him for ourselves. Bishop Bill Hamon says Jesus Christ is the brightness display of God's glory and the greatest expression of God's person ever to occur in eternity. Jesus is our model of God and connection with God. Jesus restored God's heart to our heart, and our heart to God's heart. He is the embodiment of God speaking. John 1:1 says, *"In the beginning was the Word, and the Word was with God, and the Word was God."* Jesus is the Word. He is the Word of God made flesh.

Every Believer Can Prophesy

You are on earth in the day when the truth has been restored that every believer can flow in the gifts of the Holy Spirit. You can prophesy. You can share God's voice and heart with others. Acts 2:17 reveals:

> And in the last days it shall be, God declares, that I will pour out my Spirit on **all** flesh, and your sons and your daughters shall prophesy, and your young men shall see visions, and your old men shall dream dreams.

Just in case you didn't know, we are in the last days. Oooh, spooky. Actually it's not really scary, as we have been in the last days since the day of Pentecost. Hebrews 1:2 tells us: *"but in these last days he has spoken to us by his Son, whom he appointed the heir of all things, through whom also he created the world."* And First Corinthians 14:31 says: *"For you can all prophesy one by one, so that all may learn and all be encouraged,"*

These verses confirm that prophesying is for *all* of us—not some, not the elite, not just the prophets. Every believer gets to be part of this ministry. Psalm 95:7-8 says: *"For he is our God,* and we are the people of his pasture, and the sheep of his hand. Today, if you hear his voice, do not harden your hearts...." This passage instructs us what to do when we hear His voice—*do not harden your hearts*. What does that mean? It means when He's speaking, have your heart open to receive from Him. Take in what He is saying because it is His heart for us.

Prophet Versus Prophetic People

We want to make this distinction early—being able to prophesy is not the same thing as being a prophet. Just like being able to drive a car fast is not the same as being a professional race car driver. You may or may not be a prophet, but you can still activate the prophetic to operate in your life. This book does not teach you how to be a prophet—it teaches you how to flow in the spirit of prophecy and be a prophetic believer.

The difference between a prophet and a prophetic believer is found in Ephesians 4:11-12:

> And he gave the apostles, the **prophets**, the evangelists, the shepherds and teachers, to equip the saints for the work of ministry, **for building up the body of Christ.**

The office of a prophet is a function of leadership, ordained by God to the Church for the maturing and equipping of the body of Christ. A New Testament prophet equips the body of believers to be prophetic. They have a mantle from God to release a prophetic atmosphere and environment for the prophetic to operate in the lives of believers.

To put it simply, prophets are like coaches. They train the believers to go onto the field of their life and play with all the tools God has given them access to. The coach is there to make sure you have what you need to have victory over your adversary. A fivefold prophet empowers you to take on the enemy and win. Prophet still need training to build up and sharpen their prophetic gifting also.

A prophetic person is activated in the spirit of prophecy, as Revelation 19:10 says, *"...For the testimony of Jesus is the spirit of prophecy,"* which every believer has access to by being born again and filled with the Holy Spirit. A believer activated in the prophetic can receive and share the heart of God to others.

To Serve the World

The previous moves of God were establishing hosting and highlighting the fact that we should have the presence of God in our church and services. We have now built that foundation and understand that this is very important. Now that this foundation is set, God is leading us to take it outside of our churches and service times—we must release it to the world. We are in what Bishop Bill Hamon calls "The Day of the Saints," which simply means every saint can be activated in the gifts of the Spirit and can minister God's heart to others.

We are called to minister to the world, not just to other believers. The word "minister" means to serve, which means we are called to serve the world. When we serve people, they will encounter the heart and love of God. We can serve them in many ways, but we want to highlight that we can serve them with prophetic ministry. We can give them a prophetic word that opens their hearts and connects them to God.

To Build the Church

And I tell you, you are Peter, and on this rock I will build my church, and the gates of hell shall not prevail against it (Matthew 16:18).

Jesus says, *"I will build my church."* Jesus is not talking about an institution or organization structure. He is talking about people. We are the Church. It's not about building a multilevel marketing pyramid void of connection to people.

He is building us. Each and every one of us is in whom and where He is building. First Peter 2:5 says we are living stones that are being built up as a spiritual house. He is building in our hearts. He is establishing us in the things of God. The prophetic is one of His tools to build His church.

We will define in more detail in the next chapter what prophecy is for: edification, exhortation, and comfort. The prophetic builds us up corporately as the body of Christ—and individually. When corporate words are released, it gives us direction as a unit to focus our faith on the same thing. The prophetic is like a hammer and nail. It helps to build and strengthen the body for its God-given purpose and assignment.

Desire the Prophetic

But earnestly desire the higher gifts. And I will show you a still more excellent way (1 Corinthians 12:31).

Therefore, my brothers and sisters, be eager to prophesy, and do not forbid speaking in tongues (1 Corinthians 14:39 NIV).

In these two verses, God says to desire and be eager to prophesy. God permits us to desire to prophesy. He is telling us this is a great thing to do and have in your life, so desire it. It would be like a friend telling you about a new app that cooks your dinner and cleans your house for you. Someone reading this, go invent that. I bet you will be a billionaire if you do.

First your friend starts to tell you all the benefits so that you would desire it. Then the friend tells you to download it now. God is doing the same thing. He is telling us how great this ministry is and that we should want or desire it, because it's going to be a blessing to your life.

doing prophecy is a blessing to our / my life

Don't just desire to *receive* a word. Desire to *give* a word. The Bible says in Acts 20:35 that Jesus Himself said, "*It is more blessed to give than to receive.*"

Step one to begin the prophetic flowing in your life is to desire it. Do you desire it? I think it is fair to say yes, because you're reading this book. Mark 11:24 gives us the blueprint to receiving from God: "*Therefore I tell you, whatever you ask in prayer, believe that you have received it, and it will be yours.*"

Step two is to *ask* in prayer. So, we encourage you to pray the following prayer:

> *Father, I desire to hear Your voice. I desire to share Your heart, mind, will, and thoughts to others to edify, exhort, and comfort. I want to be an extension and expression of Your hands, feet, and mouth to others. I yield my spirit to You to receive words that will be Holy Spirit-led and produce life in peoples' lives. In Jesus' name.*

Step three is *believe* that you now have it. We asked God for a gift that He desires for us to have, and He is the good Father. We know from Matthew 7:9 that He will give the good thing we're asking for: *"Or which one of you, if his son asks him for bread, will give him a stone?"* The prophetic is bread and life.

Step four is *receive*. You now have received the ability to flow in the spirit of prophecy. It's in you. The final step is to *activate* it in your life. The rest of this book will help you activate and walk in the gift that the Holy Spirit deposited in you.

Activation

Now I want you to stop, close your eyes, and hear what the Holy Spirit is saying to you. What do you hear the Holy Spirit saying to you right now? Maybe a thought flashes through your mind, it might be a feeling that you get, you might see a picture. But I know right now in this moment, the Holy Spirit is speaking to you. Focus in to listen and to receive from the Lord right now. Don't be in a rush to go to the next chapter; rather, take this moment and allow Him to start to activate the prophetic inside you.

Chapter 2

WHAT IS PROPHECY?

A team of our prophetic minsters from our church was traveling and ministering. They prophesied to a lady, and when
they were done, the lady said, "I just realized I've never been
prophesied to. I'd been *prophe-lied* to!" We thought that was the
funniest thing. Once she encountered the heart of God accurately prophesied to her, she could quickly see what she had
experienced previously was not the real thing.

Let's start with what is *not* prophecy. I have seen a lot of
well-meaning people share things and say it is prophecy. For
example, we have heard people say, "I prophesy you're getting a
new car," or, "I prophesy you're getting a check in the mail," or,
"I prophesy you're getting a new house." These statements have
become popular terminology. However, it's not biblical prophecy. Throwing the words "I prophesy" before a comment does
not make it prophecy. This is not how it works. We wish it did.
We would prophesy ourselves into all kinds of great blessings.
Wouldn't you? "We prophesy you're reading this book." What!
Yes, we know you were just amazed at that word. Wow, how did
we know that? Just kidding of course.

On a serious note, *prophesy is actually an unction led by the
Holy Spirit to release the thought, heart, and will of God.* The author
of the prophetic word is the Holy Spirit. It is Him sharing the
thoughts and intentions of God with us. It is Him sharing His
heart with us. It could be about great blessings that are about to
come into our lives. It can also be Him just letting us know that
He sees us and is there for us.

Revelation 19:10 says, *"For the testimony of Jesus is the spirit of prophecy."* That means, prophecy speaks of Jesus and reveals Jesus. A prophetic word should always point you to and connect you back to Jesus.

We have received many prophetic words in our lives. Sometimes the word is just about things we were feeling and experiencing. It was God's way of letting us know He was there and involved in the details. That brought peace and comfort to our hearts. We received the heart of God through it.

Prophetic ministry is part of your Christian life. It does not replace the Word, prayer, preaching, praise, worship, teaching, fellowship, etc. All things in your Christian life must be in right balance.

What Is the Purpose of Prophecy?

But he who prophesies speaks edification and exhortation and comfort... (1 Corinthians 14:3 NKJV).

According to this Scripture verse in First Corinthians 14, prophecy is for edification, exhortation, and comfort. Let's define these words so we can know what to expect from biblical New Testament prophecy—either when we give a word or receive a word.

"Edification" means to build up, fortified like a castle with walls around it to protect from enemies, to give you strength (Strong's Concordance 3619). So, through the prophetic word, God is going to give you strength. You will have the strength to stand against the enemy and have confidence in what God is doing in your life. The prophetic word will build you up, which means you will have more than you had before. You'll have more joy, faith, courage, boldness, love, trust, etc. More of what you need.

"Exhortation" means a calling for, summons, hence: (a) exhortation, (b) entreaty, (c) encouragement, joy, gladness, (d) consolation, comfort (Strong's Concordance 3874). So, the prophetic word is going to move you to action. It energizes you. When I get an encouragement from a friend, it motivates me. I see the friend's belief in me, which causes me to believe in myself. The prophetic word will empower you to do what the word says. It's letting you know God's got your back. Go for it. Go pursue your God-given destiny.

"Comfort" means encouragement, consolation, exhortation (Strong's Concordance 3889). This means that the prophetic word is coming into right where you are—to your pain, disappointment, rejection, sadness—bringing you peace. It's come to cheer you up. It is pulling you out of any negative place. It's like when you're sick and someone brings you your favorite food. It soothes your pain and comforts your soul.

Each one of those definitions were positive. God has positive things to say to and through you. The enemy is the one that speaks negatively. God is full of love for you. God's words come to you like a life coach, cheering you on, encouraging you, motivating you.

Sharing the heart of God with people is one of the most honoring and humbling things you can do. It's incredible to see how it impacts and changes their lives. We're so excited that you have a desire to grow in your prophetic gifting. The Holy Spirit is even more eager to use you.

Every believer activated in prophetic ministry is another soldier who has reported for duty in the army of the Lord. That person is building an army of radical believers who are fully empowered to demonstrate the Kingdom of God wherever they go. That's you! Let's create a foundation as we prepare to get you activated.

Jermaine Here

Rebecca and I were invited to minister at a prophetic conference. We met the pastor a few years before and ministered at his church and connected well. He was introduced to the prophetic and fell in love with that type of ministry. He was a pastor in a large and popular denomination, that unlike him, was not such a fan of prophecy. Nevertheless, the pastor felt led by the Lord to host a prophetic conference.

When we arrived at the conference, there were rooms set up for us where we could prophesy over all the attendees. Rebecca and I split into two teams and ministered to people like we normally do. I started sharing with a man about the desires of his heart and what he had been through, and what God's purpose was for him. He busted out with a loud wail and then uncontrollable sobbing. Then he fell on the floor and started rolling around, weeping loudly. I was excited that God was ministering to him. I moved on to the next person in line for ministry, leaving him there rolling around and weeping. I did not think much more about it.

The next day in the general session of the conference, they were getting ready to introduce us to speak. The same man got up and pointed at Rebecca and me. He said, "I have to repent, these are true prophets." He told us that he was the superintendent of the entire region for the denomination, and he came to the meeting to shut down all this prophetic stuff. He said,

"I did not believe in any of it." He decided to sneak into the prophetic rooms to see what kind of nonsense we were telling people. Then he could shut it down with evidence.

The man said, "I went in undercover. I did not dress up. I tried to be casual and hide. Then they started prophesying, and he told me word for word the conversation my wife and I had in the car on the way to the church. Jermaine said things and desires I had in my heart that I have told no one about. This thing is real. This event has my blessing."

We were stunned, and we were glad we didn't know in advance that the man was against us prophesying. God knew, but God wasn't trying to confront him. Instead, God wooed him by touching his heart in a deep and meaningful way. That's the beauty of prophecy!

The Prophetic Opens Hearts

The prophetic opens people's hearts. It connects people's hearts with God's heart for them. People who have been hurt have a hard time trusting. The prophetic can be a key to open their hearts. If they can see that God knows them and cares, it can help them. Sometimes all people need is to know that someone cares. Finding out that God cares can make the biggest impact in their lives. We all value different things based on what we have gone through and experienced in life. And God knows that and can speak right into what matters to us.

The goal of the prophetic is to connect us to God. If we are only impressed, then the true heart of God was not released or demonstrated.

God Is on a Mission

God desires to be known. He desires to know us and for us to know Him. Where the enemy has been on a mission to remove God from the earth, God is on a mission to make Himself known in every area of the earth. Why has God not been demonstrating His power on earth in a greater way already? Here is why. He has been empowering and equipping His Church to be the instrument that will do that for Him. The enemy has tried to strip the Church of its authority and power for centuries.

History of Church Restoration

Without going into a lot of historical context, we'll just give you a brief overview of why prophecy was mostly dormant in the Church until the last several decades. False teaching came in throughout church history, hiding truth from the Church. The Holy Spirit in the past 500 years has been at work restoring and releasing truth back to the body of Christ. This is an exhilarating time to be alive. You get to be on the planet as the Church steps into her maturity.

To know where we are going, let's take a look at where we have been. The Western church you currently see is not the church structure that has always been. The church had to go through a transformation process to get to its current state. The church went through a dark period between AD 500 to 1500. During this era, not much was happening spiritually in the church. There was no flowing revelation of God; rather, there were a lot of religious teachings, traditions, and dead works to earn salvation.[1]

The dark ages for the church came to an end in 1517 when Martin Luther nailed the 95 theses on the Castle Church in Wittenberg, Germany. Martin Luther had received the revelation from Romans 1:17 that the *just shall live by faith.* This revelation challenged the teachings of the church in that day, which taught salvation was earned by a person's works. His revelation birthed the understanding that salvation was by faith in Jesus Christ. It began a new era in the church, birthing the Protestant Reformation. We recently celebrated the 500-year anniversary of this movement.

In the 1600s, there was a revelation of water baptism, and many fundamental churches were formed in this time. In the 1700s was the Holiness movement, which restored sanctification for the believer. In the 1800s was the Faith Healing movement, which restored the understanding that Jesus died for our healing as well as salvation.

In the 1900s, one of the most empowering shifts for the body of Christ happened through the Pentecostal and Charismatic movements. There was an especially great outpouring that took place in 1906 on Azusa Street in Los Angeles, California, with William Seymour. The revelation of being baptized in the Holy Spirit with the evidence of speaking in tongues was released into the body of Christ. When the Holy Spirit brings forth a revelation of a truth, it builds on a previous revelation or truth, it does not do away with an earlier Holy Spirit-led revelation.

In the 1950s the Holy Spirit began to restore the office of the evangelist revealed in Ephesians 4:11. This is the era when evangelists Billy Graham, Bill Bright, Oral Roberts, William Branham, and others appeared on the scene. They held massive tent crusades where the healing and delivering power of God was on display. This brought the validation and need for the evangelist back to the church.

In the 1960s, the Holy Spirit began to restore the office of the pastor. Many large churches were built to house the many people who were saved under the office of the evangelist.

In the 1970s the Holy Spirit began to restore the office of the teacher through the faith movement. What else would you now do with a church full of new converts? They needed to be taught and discipled. During this time, it became trendy to attend Christian gatherings for the sake of hearing teachings. The practice of purchasing cassette tapes and listening to teachings was created as believers had a great desire to learn from the Word of God.

Let's keep going. The Holy Spirit is building something wonderful and you are part of it.

In the 1980s, the Holy Spirit began to restore the office of the prophet. During this period, Christian International started hosting prophetic conferences and meetings, where the main speakers of these events used the title of prophet. This was not yet normal in Christendom.

In the 1990s, the Holy Spirit began to restore the office of the apostle. During this period of time, many people started to use the title of apostle. Apostolic conferences began to take place. People such as C. Peter Wagner hosted apostolic events. Apostolic networks started to be birthed. The notoriety and the value on the title apostle grew as books were written on the subject of the apostolic.

The Holy Spirit was restoring the fivefold ministry gifts to the church. Now we can begin to move from Ephesians 4:11 to Ephesians 4:12-13 (NIV), which says:

To equip his people for works of service, so that the body of Christ may be built up until we all reach unity in the faith and in the knowledge of the Son of God and become mature, attaining to the whole measure of the fullness of Christ.

Now the Holy Spirit is activating every believer in the body of Christ to begin to function in the gifts of the Holy Spirit.

In the 2000s, the Holy Spirit is restoring the power of God to the believers. This is what we talked about earlier, that Bishop Bill Hamon calls The Day of the Saints.

Now move forward into who you are and what the Holy Spirit has for you to do in this season of Church history.

Activation

God is moving in the corporate body of Christ, but every movement starts in an individual on a local level first. I want you to partner with what God is doing in you and your local church. Take few a minutes and pray for your local church. Agree with what the Holy Spirit is doing and desires to do in you and your local church. Ask God to show you what you can practically do in the natural to partner with Him.

ENDNOTE

1. Nate Sullivan, Instructor; "The Dark Ages: Definition, History & Timeline"; Study.com; https://study.com/academy/lesson/the-dark-ages-definition-history-timeline.html; accessed May 9, 2019.

Chapter 3

ACCURACY OF
THE HEART

One of the scariest things of the prophetic, to us, is how easy it is for any believer to operate in the ministry of prophecy regardless of what else is going on in their hearts, lives, and relationship with the Lord. However, we also know that while it may seem a person can function in a gift regardless of the person's character, true prophecy is the heart of God being expressed. You can't express someone else's heart if you're not deeply connected to that person's heart yourself.

Our mentor and prophetic trainer Prophet Bill Lackie describes intimacy with Jesus as more than just transparency and closeness. It's standing face to face with Him—there's nothing hidden from His sight. Intimacy means nothing left unexposed in His presence and in light of Him. It's letting our souls be undressed before Him. And it's all the while keeping our gaze directly on Him. He is the only Source. He is the only Goal. He is the Crown Jewel of Heaven!

Prophets Who Don't Know God

People can function in the spirit of prophecy without maintaining this kind of intimacy with Jesus. We know this because Jesus said, *"Many will say to me on that day, 'Lord, Lord, did we not prophesy in your name...and perform many miracles?' Then I will tell them plainly, 'I never knew you. Away from me, you evildoers!'"*[1]

As prophets, we can't imagine a more horrifying moment. These ministers thought they were serving Jesus. They thought they were fulfilling destiny. They thought they were bringing

His Kingdom to earth. They obviously believed in Jesus and in His power. We can come up with all kinds of explanations of how these people got to the gates of Heaven only to be sent to hell. Whatever explanation we come up with might make us feel better about ourselves. But the bottom line is…there are Christian ministers who will not enter eternity with Jesus even after living their lives on earth in His name.[2]

Using the gift without intimacy doesn't mean we were never saved. It doesn't mean we never met Jesus. It could mean, though, that in some measure, our source or our focus becomes the gift rather than Jesus. It could mean that there is some end result in our mind other than Jesus, even if it's a good result, that motivates us in our gifts.

When our affection and focus is Jesus, the gift will flow out of us freely and indefinitely. We will hardly be able to contain it. And it may result in influence, or in God causing doors to open. But if we set out on a goal to gain influence or open doors through our gifts, and turn to Jesus only in order to get the gift from Him, then intimacy with Him is secondary.

Sorcery

Intimacy with Jesus is the driving force behind our gifts. Using our gifts any other way is similar to what Simon the sorcerer did.

> Now for some time a man named **Simon had practiced sorcery** in the city and amazed all the people of Samaria. He boasted that he was someone great, and all the people, both high and low, gave him their attention and exclaimed, "This man is rightly called the Great Power of God." They followed him because

*he had amazed them for a long time with his sorcery. But when they believed Philip as he proclaimed the good news of the kingdom of God and the name of Jesus Christ, they were baptized, both men and women. **Simon himself believed and was baptized. And he followed Philip everywhere, astonished by the great signs and miracles he saw.***

When the apostles in Jerusalem heard that Samaria had accepted the word of God, they sent Peter and John to Samaria. When they arrived, they prayed for the new believers there that they might receive the Holy Spirit, because the Holy Spirit had not yet come on any of them; they had simply been baptized in the name of the Lord Jesus. Then Peter and John placed their hands on them, and they received the Holy Spirit.

When Simon saw that the Spirit was given at the laying on of the apostles' hands, he offered them money and said, "Give me also this ability so that everyone on whom I lay my hands may receive the Holy Spirit."

Peter answered: "May your money perish with you, because you thought you could buy the gift of God with money! You have no part or share in this ministry, because your heart is not right before God. Repent of this wickedness and pray to the Lord in the hope that he may forgive you for having such a thought in your heart. For I see that you are full of bitterness and captive to sin."

Then Simon answered, "Pray to the Lord for me so that nothing you have said may happen to me" (Acts 8:9-24 NIV).

Simon was a Christian. The Bible says he believed and was baptized, then followed Philip everywhere, amazed by Philip's ministry. But Simon had a foundation of sorcery.

Sorcery was the general practice of the supernatural, demonstrating either supernatural powers or knowledge. It was actually quite common in those days. It was more common—prior to Pentecost—than the supernatural power of God! Simon's followers said he had great power. Simon was familiar with having leadership because of his supernatural power. He would have known how to gain influence by demonstrating his power. So when it came time for the true power of God to show up in his life, he saw it as a source of influence. He saw his next open door.

Although he was a Christian, Simon's reaction to Peter and John revealed what was still inside his heart. He was not right with God. It doesn't say that he even knew before this moment that he was not right with God. There's no indication that Philip knew. But when the moment of testing came, what was in Simon's heart surfaced.

If that moment had not happened, could Simon have said on that day, "Lord, I prophesied in Your name"? Absolutely! In God's grace, Simon had the opportunity to see what was in his own heart, and he had the opportunity to repent. We don't know what he did, but we at least know he had the opportunity to repent and be delivered of his ungodly motives.

Part of a Natural Relationship with God

All believers should have the supernatural power of God demonstrated throughout their lives. It is the overflow of our intimacy with Him.

It's just like when after worshipping, things are clearer, or what bothered you before worship didn't bother you as much after. Or how you can pray and believe for something, and when you're done, even though the problem is not solved, the issue is settled inside you. When you are close to Jesus, or when you are intimate with the Holy Spirit, He ministers to you and He opens your eyes. You can see more clearly because you've been with Him.

Rebecca Here

I remember one time when a good friend of mine was in the middle of transition. A lot was going on in her life, both good and even some not-so-good things, which is common when a lot of changes happen at once. Not everything is perfect. And I didn't expect it to be perfect. But there were some things that my friend could have adjusted to, which would have brought greater success in the middle of her transition.

I'm actually not a very confrontational person, at least when it comes to my friends, because I figure that ultimately things will work out. So in my mind when I saw the hard things my friend was dealing with, and I saw the demonic assignment against my friend, I just prayed initially and kept it to myself.

The truth is, in the spirit, the demonic assignment against my friend needed to be addressed. That was uncomfortable for me. That was not natural for me. That was not something fun or that I wanted to do at all. I felt like throwing up, my heart was racing, and I cried all night because of the intensity I felt about having to have any kind of conflict and confrontation with my dear friend. But then I took the advice of my brilliant mentor—I went to Jesus.

After some worship and connecting my heart to the heart of God, I thought about everything differently. I could see more clearly in the spirit. I knew what was at stake if I did not confront this demonic assignment. I knew the only option was to deal with the issue in the spirit, and even though it wouldn't be fun, I knew my emotions would survive. I also knew my friend would survive. Actually, I knew my friend would be better off for it!

I was able to have that very difficult discussion with my friend and we came to a place of breakthrough together, to a better unity with each other after getting closer to Jesus to deal with the issue. Deliverance came, and the prophet in me arose to the challenge with clarity, because of intimacy with Jesus. Intimacy always bring clarity in the spirit. Intimacy will bring clarity even when you're not looking for clarity, but especially when you need it!

Let's not get it upside down. Let's not want to give a good prophecy, and in doing so turn to Jesus to get that word. Instead let's turn to Him for the sake of intimacy with Him. In intimacy with Him, accuracy of His heart will come in the form of prophecy.

Accuracy of the Heart

This is a good time to talk about accuracy. When we think of accuracy in terms of the prophetic, we usually think of dates and names and details. We imagine someone who can pick a random person in the audience and get a word of knowledge about what the person's telephone number is or their aunt's middle name. And that is possible. And when that happens, it's purposeful, but that's not the actual heart of accuracy.

We have learned, first from our mentors, Prophet Bill Lackie and Dr. Bill Hamon, and then from experience, that accuracy has more to do with the heart of God than the details of the person's life. In other words, an accurate prophecy would accurately convey God's heart about a situation more importantly than it would give accurate details about the situation. We find both kinds of accuracy in our best scriptural example of the word of knowledge. By the way, the word of knowledge is simply God revealing details that weren't naturally known. This is the gift being utilized when people prophesy natural details.

When Jesus ministered to the woman at the well, which is a prominent word-of-knowledge example, He said something specific about her. He said that the man she was with was not her husband. And that she had many husbands. That is a word of knowledge. Jesus did not know that from a conversation with her, or from observing her. He knew it by the Spirit. (See John 4:1-26.)

You know what? That's not actually all that detailed or specific! Jesus did not tell her the name of the men she had been with, or the thought in her head right at the moment, or any other intensely detailed information. But He did reveal something that He could never have known in the natural, which God revealed to Him. When Jesus did that, He got her attention. He gave just enough word of knowledge details to get her attention; but getting her attention was to give her something else. He gave her God's heart.

An accurate word of knowledge or an accurate detail in prophecy is only as good as the accuracy of the heart of God that follows it. How clearly does it reveal God to the person? How accurately does it convey the counsel of God's heart, His will, His way, and His word for the person's life? That's how prophecy comes to a higher standard. That's the true standard of accuracy.

Even sorcerers can tell people details about their lives, details that actually those people already know anyway. It does little good to tell people the details of their lives unless somehow it points them to Jesus when you're done.

So do we really need to look for accurate details? Should we pursue that gift? No, we should pursue Jesus. Out of our love for Jesus, if we are willing demonstrate His gift to the church, we will also have the gifts needed to minister His heart to others. We will become the gifts He has given someone else. We will become the outpouring of His heart in their lives through the gift of prophecy.

False Prophets

This brings us to the subject of being a false prophet. Giving a word that has inaccurate information does not make you a false prophet. We are all human and can misinterpret something we receive from the Holy Spirt.

A false prophet is someone who is leading people away from God. A false prophet can have an accurate word, information, but be inaccurate at heart. The false prophet's heart and motives are not in right alignment with God. They may have their own agenda and are trying to draw people to themselves and not God. Their gift might be amazing, but their character is out of right alignment. A scriptural example is found in Numbers 22–24 where the prophet Balaam prophesied an accurate word, but was against God's agenda in his heart. We refer to Balaam more in Chapter 6.

ENDNOTES

1. Matthew 7:22-23 NIV.
2. Bishop Bill Hamon writes about this in his book, *How Can These Things Be?—A Preacher and a Miracle Worker but Denied Heaven!*, published in 2015 by Destiny Image Publishers.

WAYS TO HEAR
GOD'S VOICE

You have already been hearing God's voice more than you realize. Even if you already thought you were hearing God, I promise you can hear Him even more! The process of learning to hear God's voice is simple. Learning to recognize when you hear Him teaches you how to put meaning—or words—to something already in you.

Which came first, an object, or the object's name? It's not a trick question. The object came first. When Adam named the animals, he looked at something that existed and found language to communicate its existence.

Hearing God works the same way. He gives us meaning in our spirits. That meaning can come in a millisecond, and yet it can be full of what feels like hours or days' worth of content. That's because of a couple of things. The first and most important reason for this is that God's Spirit is eternal, and the depth of His communication to our spirit is unfathomable: *"How precious also are Your thoughts to me, O God! How great is the sum of them! If I should count them, they would be more in number than the sand..."* (Psalm 139:17-18 NKJV).

The other main reason that a second of revelation from God seems to take minutes or hours to understand and or explain has to do with the way our minds work. Our conscious minds process 4,000 actions per second. You read that right—per second! And our nonconscious minds process 4,000,000 actions per second.[1] This is the unfathomable, complex way God designed our minds.

So when God drops one second of revelation from His Spirit to our spirit, it's no surprise that it can be translated into sentences, paragraphs, and even books' worth of words. When combining the supernatural with the natural brilliance of our minds, it's possible that one second of revelation could equal anywhere from 4,000 to 4,000,000 words. Of course, 4,000,000 would be a bit of an exaggeration, but you can see that the math is at least 4,000 times the content per second of revelation.

In order to translate Spirit revelation into words, we first need to know how we're processing the revelation through our minds. We receive the revelation by our spirit. We do not receive it in our minds. We do not need to understand the revelation. We do not need to have prior knowledge about the revelation. Revelation comes from God's Spirit to our spirit regardless of our minds.

But there's a caveat. We need our minds to make sense of, meditate on, communicate, and apply the revelation.

Let's add this disclaimer before we continue. Whatever revelation you receive must be biblical. If you see and hear anything that goes against the Bible, reject it. In social media terms—unfriend it, delete it, block it, unfollow, report it. Don't connect with it at all. God never contradicts Himself.

The Theater of the Mind

Did you ever notice how sometimes reading the book is better than watching the movie? Or did you ever want to create something artistic, that you could see so clearly in your head, but by the time you draw it or construct it, it was not much better than sticks or stick figures?

What happens in our minds can be much richer than what happens in the natural world because of something called "the theater of the mind." The theater of the mind is the culmination of colors, shapes, sensations, smells, sounds, movement, multitasking, and backstory that exists in our minds. Our parents called it our "imagination."

The phrase "theater of the mind" comes from radio jargon. When people used to listen to stories on the radio, the "actors" found ways to verbally create a theater for listeners to enjoy in their minds. This is not to be confused with the contemporary New Age discussion of self-hypnosis that has recently highjacked this phrase.

The theater of the mind explains why when you have a dream, you can say that you "somehow knew" where you were or to whom you were talking, even though it was never directly identified in the dream. The theater of the mind contains indirect information that adds richness to the experience.

When God speaks to our spirit, we can experience much of that revelation in the theater of our minds.

Sight

Sight is the first aspect of the theater of the mind. This is our "mind's eye." In your mind's eye, you can see the red solo cup sitting to your right, with a sweat ring around the base and half full of ice-cold water. How did you see it, when all you are looking at is a white page with black words printed on it? You saw it in your mind's eye.

Let's call this your mind's eye rather than your imagination so that you get comfortable thinking of images you see in your mind as valid. Unfortunately, because we have called it our imagination for so long, many people who are seeing things of the spirit are clearly seeing from God—but they think they're just imagining.

We'll talk about spiritual sight more in the seer chapter. For now, let's understand this to be any visual in your mind's eye, anything you can "see" other than with your natural eyes. This could even include seeing a word, just like if I asked you right now to see the name of the street you live on.

Scripture examples of seeing include the following:

> *And Elisha prayed, and said, "Lord, I pray, open his eyes that he may see." Then the Lord opened the eyes of the young man, and he saw. And behold, the mountain was full of horses and chariots of fire all around Elisha* (2 Kings 6:17 NKJV).

> *And he said to me, "What do you see?" So I answered, "I see a flying scroll. Its length is twenty cubits and its width ten cubits"* (Zechariah 5:2 NKJV).

> *Then God spoke to Israel in the visions of the night, and said, "Jacob, Jacob!" And he said, "Here I am"* (Genesis 46:2 NKJV).

> *Then I turned to see the voice that spoke with me. And having turned I saw seven golden lampstands* (Revelation 1:12).

Sound

Sound is another element of the theater of the mind. Do you ever have a discussion in your head? This is the sound in the theater of your mind. When you have a discussion in your head, the entire thing may be in your own voice. Or occasionally, you might think something that your parents used to say, and you might think it in the sound of your mother's voice.

Sound also includes tone, inflection, intensity, and pitch, which is how you might be able to tell whether something said was sarcastic or supportive, harsh or gentle. "You will always be mine" could sound endearing, romantic, apologetic, or like a stalker, all depending on how it's said.

Scripture examples of hearing:

> *Now the Lord came and stood and called as at other times, "Samuel! Samuel!" And Samuel answered, "Speak, for Your servant hears"* (1 Samuel 3:10 NKJV).

> *Also I heard the voice of the Lord, saying: "Whom shall I send, and who will go for Us?" Then I said, "Here am I! Send me"* (Isaiah 6:8 NKJV).

> *And they heard the sound of the Lord God walking in the garden in the cool of the day, and Adam and his wife hid themselves from the presence of the Lord God among the trees of the garden* (Genesis 3:8 NKJV).

> *Did any people ever hear the voice of God speaking out of the midst of the fire, as you have heard, and live?* (Deuteronomy 4:33 NKJV).

Sensing

Sensing has to do with how something feels in the theater of your mind. Sensing may be informed by the other elements, such as sound and sight, but it can also stand apart from them.

You might have an interaction with an old friend in public somewhere. During the interaction, you might get the sense that your friend is in a hurry, or that he or she doesn't want to go too in depth in their discussion with you. You could get that sensing from their body language or how brief their answers to your questions are, but you could also get that sensing without any other input.

Sensings are sometimes called a "gut feeling." These aren't necessarily emotions but rather feelings or sensings that give us information. A sensing is where you might identify, for example, whether a purple cloud-like presence in your dream was positive rather than negative. You may not have any other point of reference for that weird, dreamworld image, but your gut feeling about it gave you the sense that it was good.

We often get a "sense" about situations and people in the real world. Sensings in the theater of the mind work the same way.

Scripture examples of sensing or feeling:

> *Then Jesus was led up by the Spirit into the wilderness to be tempted by the devil* (Matthew 4:1 NKJV).

> *In the same way, the Spirit helps us in our weakness. We do not know what we ought to pray for, but the Spirit himself intercedes for us through wordless groans. And he who searches our hearts knows the mind of the Spirit, because the Spirit intercedes for God's people in accordance with the will of God* (Romans 8:26-27 NIV).

Verse Concepts

> *If we live in the Spirit, let us also walk in the Spirit* (Galatians 5:25 NKJV).

Immediately the Spirit drove Him into the wilderness
(Mark 1:12 NKJV).

Knowing

Knowing is an interesting aspect of the theater of the mind.
Knowing includes backstory that is never explained. Just like
in the dream mentioned earlier—when you knew where you
were or to whom you were talking, without it being mentioned
in the dream—knowing is information you have without any
direct source.

When you "know" in the theater of your mind, you often
can't explain why you know. This kind of knowing is hard to
defend. It's similar to a sensing, except that it usually doesn't
even have an emotion or inclination to support it. All you have
is the thing you know that you know, even though you don't
know how you know it.

Scripture examples of knowing:

> *This is what we speak, not in words taught us by
> human wisdom but in words taught by the Spirit,
> explaining spiritual realities with Spirit-taught words*
> (1 Corinthians 2:13 NIV).

> *But when He, the Spirit of truth, comes, he will guide
> you into all the truth. He will not speak on his own;
> he will speak only what he hears, and he will tell you
> what is yet to come* (John 16:13 NIV).

> *And when Jesus went out He saw a great multitude;
> and He was moved with compassion for them, and
> healed their sick* (Matthew 14:14 NKJV).

Rebecca Here

I like to avoid the early morning flight when we go on ministry trips, but occasionally we book them out of necessity. One time we had the early flight out, but by the time we boarded the plane, our airline app notified us that the flight was delayed 30 minutes. Instantly, I just knew it was delayed much longer than that.

We waited 30 minutes, and then the flight attendant announced it was delayed another 30 minutes. Again I had an instant feeling that it would be delayed much longer. I told Jermaine, and we decided to get off the plane. We booked the next flight, which was at noon! We were not going to make our first speaking engagement that night if we took the noon flight, but somehow, I knew it was best.

We left the airport and went to breakfast. When we returned to the airport at 11:00, we saw our original plane, with all the passengers still on board. That flight didn't take off until 11:45, with announcements every 30 minutes that it was delayed another 30 minutes. If we hadn't had the "knowing" that this flight wasn't going anywhere, we would have waited on the tarmac, without air conditioning, for more than four hours.

It's such a little thing, but to me, it meant a lot to be liberated to have a lovely breakfast with Jermaine rather than a sweaty wait in an airplane seat. There was no evidence for the knowing, no emotion with it, and certainly no logic, but I've had enough of those knowings to learn to recognize they're more than just a random thought. That is what will develop in you too when by reason of use you train your senses to know what God is speaking to you.

A Quick Test

Let's start by figuring out some of the easiest ways you identify what God is saying to you. You could identify what God is saying in any or all of the ways cited: sight, sound, sense, or knowing. But at least one of these ways is probably easier to you than the others.

We all think in the theater of our minds, but we all think most comfortably in at least one of these ways. This is where we get the idea of learning styles: auditory learning versus visual versus kinetic, and so on. This is how you process information.

So we're going to take a simple test to determine at least one way that you comfortably process information. Remember, God wants to speak to you in a way that you will understand. He's not trying to overcomplicate it, so we won't either. Let's assume that God wants to speak to you in the easiest way for you to process the information.

Are you ready for the test? I'm going to put the test at the end of this paragraph, and I don't want you to read on until you've finished the test. Take enough time to pause and answer the question before accidentally reading on. Here is the question: What is your name?

Did you answer the question?

Great, you answered the question! I don't need to know your name—though you can email me and I'd love to chat about how this went for you! I asked your name so that you can *think* the answer.

Now let's examine how you thought the answer. Choose the one that is most true. Did you:

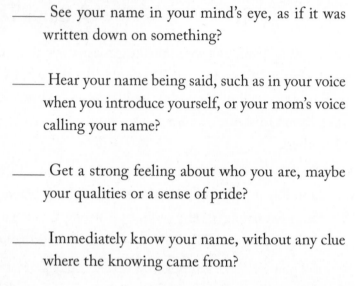

_____ See your name in your mind's eye, as if it was written down on something?

_____ Hear your name being said, such as in your voice when you introduce yourself, or your mom's voice calling your name?

_____ Get a strong feeling about who you are, maybe your qualities or a sense of pride?

_____ Immediately know your name, without any clue where the knowing came from?

Each answer represents sight, sound, sensing, and knowing, respectively. You may have had more than one of these as a reaction to the question, "What is your name." If you had more than one, that's okay and is quite common. If you don't know which one was your reaction, it was probably the last one—knowing.

Now you have a real-time example of how the theater of your mind processes information. You already know your name, but you had to think your name in reaction to the question. Similarly, when you receive revelation by the Spirit of God, you have it in your spirit, but you will have to think about the revelation using your mind to convey it effectively to other people, or even to continue to meditate on it yourself.

ENDNOTE

1. Carolyn Leaf, _Switch on Your Brain—The Key to Peak Happiness, Thinking, and Health_ (Ada, MI: Baker Books, 2015).

Chapter 5

TURN SENSINGS INTO PROPHECY

Rebecca Here

I remember the most disappointing prophecy I ever received. It sounds harsh to call a prophecy disappointing, but it was.

A prophet was getting ready to minister to me. He was experienced, and I had heard other people say they received wonderful prophecies from him. I was also new to receiving personal prophecy, so I was excited and nervous.

When this man stood in front of me, he swayed back and forth with his eyes closed and a childish grin on his face. He looked genuinely happy! He kept making happy "hmm" sounds and giggled for few seconds. Then with his eyes still shut and a lot of gestures to match his words, he said, "You're a butterfly. Flutter, flutter, flutter. You're fluttering by, you butterfly." Then he looked at me, laughed, and said, "God is so amazing," and walked away.

I couldn't believe it was over. What did that even mean? First, I was a little jealous of the experience the guy had. He looked so happy! Whatever he saw or felt, it was awesome. But what I heard was a few words that seemed nonsensical to me. I felt ripped off. Of course I tried looking up symbolisms of butterflies and praying for interpretation of this much-anticipated prophecy, but ultimately I got very little out of it. He had a great time in the presence of God, and I felt left out and unspiritual.

About ten years later I understood that situation better when I received another prophecy. Jermaine and I visited a prophet we trusted for counsel about a decision we were making together.

While talking, the prophet suddenly turned to Jermaine and said, "Your wife's heart is like a butterfly. She flutters in and out of topics like a butterfly flutters between blooms, and it may seem shallow to you, but she flutters in with all her heart, full of life and joy, open on display. Be careful not to dismiss her fluttering, it could be like closing your hand on a butterfly."

Both Jermaine and I immediately understood what he meant because we know what I'm like—how I come home and talk about 35 different topics in less than an hour, and how I'm full-force with all of my passion on each and every topic. It's so different from the way Jermaine communicates, so we've learned to adapt to each other.

That prophecy meant so much to me, because God cared about the way I approach connecting with my husband—like a butterfly fluttering around dozens of blooms. That's really what I'm like sometimes! I still well up with feelings of being understood when I remember that prophecy.

When I heard that prophecy, at the same time I could picture that man ten years earlier, with his eyes closed and a pleasant smile, humming and rocking back and forth. He saw the butterfly that I was. He felt God's joy about me, maybe even my own joy about the things I get excited and passionate over. He felt it all, but he wasn't able to communicate any of it to me.

The challenge with the first prophecy was not my level of spirituality or ability to understand God's message. The challenge was the prophet's ability to use his words to communicate what he experienced in the theater of his mind. It was simple lack of experience on his part.

It's easy to see which prophecy was more effective for me, although both were about the exact same thing. Both prophets might have even seen, heard, or sensed the same thing, but one prophet had developed the skills to communicate with words what he experienced internally by the spirit.

Develop the skills to communicate what God shows you. It will be worth it for the person with whom you share the prophecy.

Converting Theater into Prophecy

What you sense from God must be communicated effectively. Think of it like preparing a meal for guests. When your guests eat, if you've done your job well, all they experience is a delicious and well-rounded meal. They may know you did a lot of work to get it there, but they don't experience the work. They just experience the meal.

When you make a meal for someone, you get clarity about what you're going to serve, go to the grocery store and select the best options, bring it all home and wash, cut, portion, season, and prepare it, cook it, plate it, and finally serve it. The part the guest cares about is the serving, but you did a lot of background work taking those raw ingredients and turning them into a delectable and nourishing meal.

Ministry is the same way. In case you didn't catch on, prophecy is ministry. Sharing God's heart for another person is ministry. They get a lovely meal—the heart of God nourishing and giving them joy. But you do the work of preparing that meal. You serve them by prophesying.

When you minister or prophesy, you get the raw ingredients from God. You get the meat—the maturing and growing thing God wants for the person. You get the seasoning—the particular flavor and aspects that make it pleasant. And you do the work of assembling it in such a way that it's palatable. Sure, a person could eat just plain chicken breast, unseasoned, maybe boiled, and it would meet some of the body's needs. But that would be awful. What God gives you for another person is for their good, including making it palatable to receive and be nourished by it.

So let's take what you know about the theater of the mind and apply it to prophecy. Remember, prophecy is communicating what God gives you in revelation. First, you get revelation in your spirit, it unfolds, or makes sense or is otherwise converted, into the theater of your mind, and you choose words to package it up and give it to someone else.

We'll talk more about this in Chapter 9. Some things are "better caught than taught" as they say, so let's just start practicing and catch what this means. Then we'll come back and understand it more thoroughly after you have a grid.

Let's practice!

Activation

First, ask God to show you a picture from Him right now. Remember, you might "see" the picture in your mind's eye, the thing you spent most of your life calling an "imagination." You're not going to use your imagination to conjure up something yourself, but when God puts something in your spirit and you understand it in the form of a picture, it could look just like your imagination.

Got your picture? Take a minute to jot down what it is. Here's an example of a picture Rebecca received during a similar activation:

My picture is of a vase.

Now really look at the picture. Make note of anything you see.

The picture had movement, sort of like a GIF. The movement was like the vase appeared starting from bottom to top. But I noticed the GIF didn't quite finish, so I never got the whole top of the vase. It's a pretty vase.

Now ask God to give you a sense about the picture. This will be some sort of impression, or feeling, or maybe even a discernment about the picture. You might have instantly gotten the sense when you saw the picture, but if not, get a sense now.

My sense about the picture was that it is good. I did get that sense instantly. Then I asked God for a second sense, which was of anxiety.

_____

_____

_____

Now ask God to give you one word about the picture, and make a note of it.

The word God gave me is "hope."

_____

_____

_____

_____

_____

Now, is there anything you just know about the picture? If not, ask God for more about the picture now, and jot it down too.

I knew the picture not being finished was speaking to me about my expectations of myself, that God is working a process so I don't need to look so hard for an end result.

_____

_____

_____

_____

_____

Okay, let's put it all together. You now have a picture, a sense of the value of the picture, a word to go with the picture, and anything else you knew about it. Combine it all into one sentence or paragraph. At this step, don't add to it or take away. Don't try to make sense of it other than to combine what is there from God. Just combine it. You can rephrase it to make more sense now that you have each piece. The following is Rebecca's compilation.

A vase is being formed in a process. It's not done all at once. The process is good. There is hope and anticipation.

_____

_____

_____

_____

_____

Congratulations! You've used the full theater of your mind to identify something God's Spirit revealed to your spirit. This is no small thing. This is exactly how you walk by the Spirit, minister to others, and become God's instrument in the earth.

Now let's take that revelation and repackage it in a way that could minister more effectively to another person. Let's do this by asking ourselves—or better yet, God—some questions. The following questions are based on Rebecca's example. Read what she wrote, and then make your own list of questions based on your picture, word, sensing, and knowing. You will get the answers to the questions from your own sensing as you ask God each question.

Why the vase?

The vase represents something being worked on or created.

Why does this person need to hear about the process?

This person is in a process of something in them or in their life being created.

How does this person feel about the process?

This person feels anxiety because he/she wants to make sure it's finished well.

How does God want this person to feel about the process?

God wants this person to have hope.

What is God's purpose in bringing up this issue?

God is bringing up this issue because the person is stuck on getting the end result, but God is focused on the process. When the person focuses on the process, he/she will have hope from God about it.

Take a minute and write your questions. They can be very similar to the questions you just read, especially the last question.

_____

_____

_____

_____

_____

_____

_____

_____

_____

Now sense from God the answer to each question, and write it out:

_____

_____

_____

_____

_____

_____

_____

_____

Great job! After a little practice, you will do this process in your head in a matter of seconds. This is the process of converting revelation that comes to your spirit into revelation that you can deposit in someone else.

We've got one more step.

Thanks to God's answers to your questions about the revelation He gave you, you now have the intent behind the revelation and more understanding of it. You have what you need to deliver this revelation to the person it's meant to touch.

Convert the sentences you wrote into a prophecy. You'll do this by rephrasing it. Rather than phrasing it as answers to a question, you'll phrase it from the first-person perspective of God Himself. Let's use Rebecca's revelation as an example.

Here is the revelation as it came in response to each question:

- The vase represents something being created.

- This person is in a process of something in them or in the person's life being created.

- This person feels anxiety because he/she wants to make sure it's finished well.

- God wants this person to have hope.

- God is bringing up this issue because the person is stuck on getting the end result, but God is focused on the process. When the person embraces the process, he/she will have hope from God about it.

Now here it is rephrased into the first-person perspective of God speaking: My child, I have put you in a process to create something new inside of you. I'm making a good thing in your life right now, and I'm removing the anxiety about how it will turn out. As you rest in My process for you, you will be filled with hope and you will see how quickly I'm working on your behalf.

What do you think? Can you see each of the answers to the questions in the prophecy, as well the initial picture, word, sensing, and knowing?

Now it's your turn. Take a deep breath. Relax. This is basically what you did in grade school when you had to take a paragraph and rephrase it in your own words. All the content you need for the prophecy is already written out. Now just reconceptualize it as a brief and concise message from God to this person.

_____

_____

_____

_____

_____

_____

_____

_____

_____

Chapter 6

SEEING PLUS
DISCERNING

Wherever we train people in prophecy, we are asked a lot of questions about seeing. It's worth discussing further than the other methods of hearing God because it can be the most challenging to understand and interpret, as well as the most misunderstood source of revelation.

What Is "Seeing"?

Seeing prophetically can include any of the following:

- Having an image in your mind's eye, also known as your imagination

- Having a moving image, like a movie or a scene unfolding, in your mind's eye

- Seeing something as though it is physically present—where you might say, "It looked so real that I thought I could reach out and touch it."

- Having a dream

- Having a vision

- Seeing the presence of supernatural activity, such as angels or spiritual elements

One of the misconceptions about seeing in the spirit, or the seer prophet, is that the gift or experience of seeing must be tangible. In other words, people sometimes assume a seer must have the thing they see show up physically. This is a misconception that prevents many people—who are able to see in the spirit—from recognizing or acting in faith on what they see.

Elisha had an experience where he saw in the spirit, and he activated his servant to see what he was seeing.

> *When the servant of the man of God rose early in the morning and went out, behold, an army with horses and chariots was all around the city. And the servant said, "Alas, my master! What shall we do?" He said, "Do not be afraid, for those who are with us are more than those who are with them."* **Then Elisha prayed and said, "O Lord, please open his eyes that he may see." So the Lord opened the eyes of the young man, and he saw, and behold, the mountain was full of horses and chariots of fire all around Elisha.** *And when the Syrians came down against him, Elisha prayed to the Lord and said, "Please strike this people with blindness." So he struck them with blindness in accordance with the prayer of Elisha. And Elisha said to them, "This is not the way, and this is not the city. Follow me, and I will bring you to the man whom you seek." And he led them to Samaria* (2 Kings 6:15-19).

Here's what we can take away from this story regarding the ability to see prophetically or to see the supernatural realm. The prophet prays for his servant's eyes to be open to see. Before his eyes are open, thousands of angels surrounded him. The servant was totally unaware of the angels. This tells us the angels did not show up in physical form. In other words, this would not be an experience where the angel was touchable. There are plenty of examples in Scripture where angels appear in a physical form, as though they could be touched. This has little to do with the ability to see in the spirit, as this is a sovereign experience initiated by the angel, or more accurately, by God who sent the angel.

We cannot, or at least should not, provoke angels to initiate a physical appearing or interaction with us. However, we can initiate our spiritual eyes to be open to see the angels that are already present, for the purposes of God, to see what they are doing, to see what kind of spiritual atmosphere is in the room, and so on.

Balaam was another prophet who saw in the spirit. It was a strange situation because the angel was standing there when Balaam did not see him. Yet the angel could have killed Balaam. Is it possible a spiritual being that is not present in physical form could cause a physical thing like death? Well yes, of course, because that is what was about to happen to Balaam.

Then God's anger was aroused because he went, and the Angel of the Lord took His stand in the way as an adversary against him. And he was riding on his donkey, and his two servants were with him. Now the donkey saw the Angel of the Lord standing in the way with His drawn sword in His hand, and the donkey turned aside out of the way and went into the field. So Balaam struck the donkey to turn her back onto the road. Then the Angel of the Lord stood in a narrow path between the vineyards, with a wall on this side and a wall on that side. And when the donkey saw the Angel of the Lord, she pushed herself against the wall and crushed Balaam's foot against the wall; so he struck her again. Then the Angel of the Lord went further, and stood in a narrow place where there was no way to turn either to the right hand or to the left. And when the donkey saw the Angel of the Lord, she lay down under Balaam; so Balaam's anger was aroused, and he struck the donkey with his staff.

Then the Lord opened the mouth of the donkey, and she said to Balaam, "What have I done to you, that you have struck me these three times?"

And Balaam said to the donkey, "Because you have abused me. I wish there were a sword in my hand, for now I would kill you!"

So the donkey said to Balaam, "Am I not your donkey on which you have ridden, ever since I became yours, to this day? Was I ever disposed to do this to you?"

And he said, "No."

Then the Lord opened Balaam's eyes, and he saw the Angel of the Lord standing in the way with His drawn sword in His hand; and he bowed his head and fell flat on his face. And the Angel of the Lord said to him, "Why have you struck your donkey these three times? Behold, I have come out to stand against you, because your way is perverse before Me. The donkey saw Me and turned aside from Me these three times. If she had not turned aside from Me, surely I would also have killed you by now, and let her live" (Numbers 22:22-33 NKJV).

Balaam was not considered a seer prophet. This is the only time we know of him seeing a spiritual being. Yet he did not pray or choose to see it. God sovereignly opened Balaam's eyes because otherwise Balaam would have died. In God's mercy, He let Balaam see before letting him die.

Balaam could have asked to see what was going on, just like Elisha asked for his servant to see. Who knows whether or not Balaam knew this was an option, because he didn't ask; but we know that if one person could do it, another could have also.

From comparing the story of Elisha to the story of Balaam, we learn a valuable lesson—we should want to see in the spirit, and we should ask to see in the spirit.

Seeing spiritual things requires us to know what to do with what we see. Should we tell people about our experiences? Should we tell the person involved in what we saw? What do the things that we're seeing mean?

The short answers are that everything we see is for us to pray about above anything else; and we can ask God for understanding about anything we see, and He will give it to us.

Rebecca Here

Many times while growing up I would imagine scary things either at random or in my dreams. I was afraid of almost everything when I was awake. When asleep, I had at least one but often several nightmares each night.

For example, after learning in elementary school that opossums had sharp teeth and that hippopotamuses were cute in cartoons but could be aggressive in real life, I was afraid to go to bed next to the wall. Pretty weird right? But I would imagine that an opossum or hippopotamus was about to bite through the wall and eat me. My bed was up against the wall, so I slept on the edge of my bed as far from the wall as I could. I had a vivid imagination.

I also had a gift of discernment and could see in the spirit, though I didn't know what that was. Sometimes I saw shapes or colors enter the room, or beings both pleasant and unpleasant. The night that our Dalmatian, Cole, died unexpectedly, when I was just about ten years old, I was sleeping in my mom's bed with her and had seen a shadowy being come stand in her bedroom doorway. Terrified, I pulled the covers over my head and prayed the prayers my parents had taught me to pray. I somehow knew that the being went outside into the backyard. The next morning, as soon as I woke up, I found my mom to ask her to check on the dog. She responded that she had already gone out to feed Cole, and that unfortunately she found him deceased.

I told Mom what had happened the night before. She also talked to Dad on the phone that morning, who was working out of the country at the time. Dad explained that during the same hours, which were daytime for him, he had an urgency to pray against death. His work involved risks, so he prayed for himself and his team. He then felt led to pray for our family.

Dad told Mom something to the effect that he had prayed for himself and for each of us, but he didn't think to pray for our dog, Cole. I thought to myself, I didn't pray for Cole either. At that moment, I gained even more fear about the things of the supernatural, though I could rarely tell the difference between the supernatural and my own imagination.

My parents prayed for me every night about my fearful imagination and about the nightmares I would have. They taught me to quote Scriptures, like "God hasn't given me a spirit of fear, but of power, love and a sound mind,"[1] or "There is no fear in love, because perfect love casts out fear,"[2] and "More are those who are for us than those who are against us."[3]

It didn't always help. I was honestly tormented by my imagination way into my adult life. I often lost sleep, slept with a light on, and or would keep music playing or the television on to distract my imagination. Sometimes I just kept myself awake until the sun came up, then went to sleep safely in the daylight.

One day in Bible college, Jane Hamon taught a class on discernment. She explained that many people shut down their discernment because the enemy uses it to bring fear. She said fear never has to be part of our gift to see with our spiritual eyes and to discern, and that if we were experiencing fear, we should be delivered from torment and ask God to open our eyes again.

I knew she was talking to me. As a child I had seen angels and discerned and seen both wonderful and difficult things, but as an adult I saw very little in the spirit, and this was the answer to reawakening my gifts. I went in line for Jane Hamon to pray for me. When she prayed and broke the assignment of fear, instantly I felt free. But even more so, that night was the first night I did not have a nightmare in as long as I could remember. I went on to almost never have another nightmare since that day over a decade ago!

If you have struggled with any fear or torment, I want to pray for you to be free from it, so that you can gladly look with your spiritual eyes wide open to see what is happening in the spirit. Let's pray now.

> *Father, I thank You for this reader. Thank You that fear is not from You because fear has to do with torment. Thank You that Your perfect love casts out fear. Thank You that You love this precious person dearly. So in the name of Jesus, I take authority over fear and I command it to leave this person. Fear, the*

blood of Jesus has overcome you! You must go back to the tormenter from where you came because you have no place in this person's thought life any longer. I decree perfect love is filling this reader's heart where fear used to be present. Thank You, Lord, that angels are on assignment around this person, and that there are twice as many angels as any darkness. Thank You that more are they who are for us than they who are against us. Amen.

Since seeing is simply a way to receive revelation, we know that seeing can actually be a function of several of the gifts of the Spirit, specifically the gifts of prophecy, words of knowledge, and discernment.

ENDNOTES

1. 2 Timothy 1:7.
2. 1 John 4:18.
3. 2 Kings 6:16.

Chapter 7

DISCERNMENT

Discernment is one of the nine gifts of the Spirit, and it's one that can come with the ability to see.

Discerning of spirits simply means to discern the spiritual nature and state of anything, whether good, evil, or neutral; whether it's from the spirit realm or even from a human. So, you can discern the condition of a person, or what is present in any given environment, or even yourself and the sources of thoughts and feelings that come to you.

Before we discuss discerning different things, let's talk about how to handle seemingly negative discernment.

Negative Versus Positive

Jane Hamon often says that it doesn't take discernment to find something wrong. In fact, it's easy to find things that are wrong. The best person at finding, in addition to fabricating, what is wrong is satan. He is the accuser of believers.[1] So being able to know what's wrong isn't necessarily a function of any of the gifts of the Spirit, as it could as much be a function of listening to the accusations of satan against other believers, or even against ourselves.

On the contrary, to discern in its highest purpose is to discern the good. Jesus said I only do what I see my Father in Heaven doing.[2] Jesus had to actually be able to see what God was doing! He had to be able to do this by discerning, sensing, hearing, seeing. What God was doing was good. God also revealed to Jesus the plans of the enemy, since Jesus knew that

Judas was going to betray him, but the plans of the enemy did not motivate Jesus' actions. The plans of God did.

The gift of discernment, just like the gift of prophecy, can cause us to see in the spirit. It should cause us to see what God is doing and what He wants to do. It could also cause us to know what angels are doing, what aspects of God's nature are manifesting in a room, what the Holy Spirit is doing among the people in the room, what God's purpose is, and so forth.

So what should you do if you discern something negative? Follow the example of Elijah. Ask God to show you His side of the story—His purpose, what He's doing, His angels, and His presence.

Discerning People

We can discern what is going on with people, what spirit they are operating in, what source their behavior or words may be coming from, or simply their condition. If we do discern such things about people, it is to serve them and build them up.

One of the most powerful reasons to discern people is to approach them the way Jesus would approach them. The Bible says a bruised reed he will not break and a smoldering wick He will not snuff out.[3]

Rebecca Here

One time in Bible college I went to hear a speaker who was visiting our school. He was young and charismatic, and kind of a funny guy. I knew him casually through some acquaintances but didn't know much about him. When he got up to speak, as soon as he took the microphone, I saw the strangest thing.

In my mind's eye, his face turned into the face of a hog. It was wearing lots of gold rings in its nose and ears, and it looked exaggerated, kind of like a painting or a cartoon. It was not a realistic-looking hog.

This sight was so irritating to me. I could barely focus on what the speaker was saying because of how gross this vision looked, and how weird it was. I didn't like it. I got up and left the sanctuary.

Out in the church foyer, the dean of my Bible college noticed me standing around. This was before smart phones, so I was literally just standing there doing nothing. She asked me what was wrong. I don't know how she knew something was wrong, but since I was a student and she was the dean, I felt comfortable to tell her exactly why I was standing in the foyer.

My dean was unfazed by what I told her. Instead of any shock or strange reaction, without a blink, she just asked, "Oh, what does the hog mean?" It didn't cross my mind to ask that question, but immediately I thought it was perversion. So I answered "I think its perversion."

Then she said, "Perversion of what?"

I thought, *Well, it's just his head and not his whole body.* "It feels like perverse thoughts," I said.

She then asked about the gold rings. I felt like these marked achievements that were hiding the perversion, as if this spirit wanted to convince the person to achieve enough good to outweigh or disguise the bad. My dean encouraged me to pray for the speaker, and of course, to go back inside and listen to the message, trusting God to still minister to me through the message regardless of any challenges the speaker may be dealing with.

That I know of, the dean didn't do anything with the discernment I shared with her, other than pray. And rightly so, as we'll discuss more later. But I never forgot it. It was just so weird to me.

Shortly after, when this same young man approached me to start a romantic relationship, I was single at the time, I remembered that image I saw and decided against entering a relationship with him.

About a year later, I learned of some challenges in this guy's life that I was grateful to have avoided.

God didn't tell me his struggles, that would have been none of my business. But He did allow me to see something that warned me before it could have affected me negatively.

When you can see in the spirit, you can see. You can see sometimes even when you don't want to. It doesn't mean you can see everyone's issues, but it does mean some things are visible for a reason. I personally believe the things that are visible are either an assignment for us to pray for or a warning for us. However, as we will discuss in the protocols chapter, the things we see are never for gossip or to give us a reason to treat anyone less than the best God would treat them. Discernment is always to build God's Kingdom.

Discerning Places

Discerning places is both fun and purposeful. You can discern the spiritual activity anywhere—at church, work, home, in a retail store, anywhere you go. By activating your gifts, you can see and sense what God is doing.

When you enter a room, do you typically look around? Most of us assess the room—who is there, where things are in the room such as the windows, doors, seating, and maybe a snack table. We can do the same in the spirit. Any place we enter, we can open our spiritual eyes and see what is in that room. How is God's presence manifesting in the room? What angels are in the room, and what are they doing? Why are they there? What darkness may have come in the room? While you're discerning it, go ahead and cast it out since you have authority to do so.

Seeing the spiritual activity in any given room gives you the ability to agree with what God wants to do and resist anything that the enemy wants to do. As a prophetic person—which hopefully you realize that you are or you wouldn't have read this far in the book—you will quickly learn that nothing in your life is really about you.

Here's an example. Have you ever agreed to go to an event, and then for whatever reason you just didn't want to go, you were too tired, it was too hard to get there, or you didn't care anymore even though you had agreed? Then maybe you went anyway, and when you got there you met up with friends, the host, or someone else who also had a hard time making up their mind about whether or not to attend. They felt tired, or it was too far, or they just didn't care anymore. Why did you both feel the same way about the event?

Some might blame the event at this point, but prophetic people learn that much of what they experience is not as much about them as it is prophetic. In the case of this event, the experience could likely have been discernment about what another was feeling. Maybe it was discernment about how the host of the event felt—tired and overworked, or maybe burnt out.

Usually it's hindsight that shows us we weren't feeling something for ourselves but rather for other people. But with a little practice, we can learn to recognize that we are discerning while it is happening, so that we know what to do with it.

In the example of the event, the enemy may have planned to wear out those who were attending. By realizing the feelings you had were discernment about where you were going, you can then pray against the plans of the enemy and pray for God to refresh and strengthen all those associated with the event. You can also choose not to accept the weariness or difficulty as your own, shake it off, and go to the event with joy and celebration, bringing God's atmosphere in where they enemy wanted to bring darkness.

See how fun and rewarding discernment can be when you learn to use it to bring God's agenda with you?

Discerning Yourself

Discerning yourself can be the most challenging discernment, but it is worthwhile to practice. When you discern yourself, you may discern the source of thoughts and feelings that you're having, or the way God is manifesting through you today, or the assignment the enemy wants to bring against you today, and whether or not you've partnered with it.

Have you ever checked the oil level in your car? It's called a dipstick test. You take the dipstick—a long metal wire—and insert it down a tube that leads into the oil tank. When you pull the dipstick back out, oil is on the end of it. The end also has markers, so you can measure how high the oil goes on the dipstick to know how much oil is in the tank.

Discerning yourself is like doing a dipstick test. Look inside. You'll see how much oil is in there. Other than oil, whatever else is going on should be apparent to you too when you open your spiritual eyes to see and discern, and open your heart to God.

You may feel exhausted or resistant to something. Don't just sit there feeling resistant and worn out. Discern yourself. Sense what spiritual condition, need, or activity is the cause. Perhaps you're feeling exhausted because actually you feel dry, needing to feel God's touch of His presence to fill you up with joy and strength. By discerning the cause of your exhaustion, you now know exactly what to do to remedy it. You can open your heart and ask God to touch you with His presence, then receive His touch and let the exhaustion and dryness melt away.

Summary and Activation

Seeing spiritual things through the gifts of the Spirit is available to all of us. You do not have to be labeled a "seer prophet" in order to open your spiritual eyes. You also do not need to have tangible physical encounters with spiritual beings to be seeing in the spirit. All you need is to activate, open your spiritual eyes, and look.

Let's pray this prayer to open your eyes to see in the spirit.

First, please pray this prayer:

> *Father, I want to see what You are doing in Heaven like Jesus did. I want to have eyes to see You and see circumstances as You see them. I ask You to give me the gift of discernment and open my eyes to see in the spirit. I ask for the spirit of revelation. Thank You that whatever I ask in Your name, I believe I have and I will receive, in Jesus' name.*

Now I'll pray for you:

Father, thank You for this reader who desires open eyes to see what Your Spirit is doing. God, I ask You for this person's eyes to be opened. I decree eyes to see what the Spirit of God is doing. I decree open visions of God's supernatural realm. I release visions of angels, of Heaven, and of the good things of God's Kingdom. I release dreams from Heaven, and I decree this reader will have eyes to see at least twice as much good as evil, with no fear and no torment, from this day forward in Jesus' mighty name!

ENDNOTES

1. Revelation 12:10 NIV.
2. John 5:19.
3. Isaiah 42:3 NIV.

Chapter 8

SEPARATING THE SOUL AND SPIRIT

Jermaine Here

I remember prophesying to someone I knew. I had my own thoughts and opinions about this person that were based on what I had seen and conclusions I made. However, once I started to prophesy to the person, the opposite of what were my personal thoughts and beliefs were coming out of my mouth.

As I was hearing the prophetic word for the person, I realized, *Wow, God sees this person in a totally different way from how I see.* It that moment, I could see and feel the heart of God for this individual—which I must admit was a lot different from my heart for the person. However, in the prophesying process, I learned to follow God and not myself. I did not let my own thoughts affect me, and I submitted to the Spirit of God to release His thoughts. My thoughts are weak and feeble and will profit nothing in someone's life compared to the very thoughts of God for them.

Rebecca and I were invited by a youth pastor to speak at a youth event at a church. At the end of service, Rebecca and I divided the room into two groups of people and started prophesying to everyone. There were about 40 people there, most of whom we were prophesying to were young people. A few older people came in at the end of the line. I prophesied over this one guy not knowing who he was. He started weeping and shaking. Later on I found out he was the senior pastor of the church. He said, "I saw all these kids getting touched. I wanted to know what they were experiencing. The word you gave me described my vision and heart exactly."

I did not know who this man was with my natural mind or understanding. I had never met the pastor of the church since the youth pastor was the one who brought me in. I was led by the Spirit to release that word to him, not my soul. We must learn to discern between soul and spirit when we prophecy.

Separating the Soul and Spirit Is Necessary to Prophesy Accurately

Our soul is made up of three parts—our mind, will, and emotions. The soul realm is where our thoughts flow. It is also where our desires and needs live. Our soul houses our perception of things. How we view the world, people, and ourselves. It's also where we store our knowledge. Our knowledge is an accumulation of our experiences. We gather it from what we have read, what we heard from others, personally witnessed, and from our culture, families, friends, churches, etc. Our soul is the place where we come to our own wisdom and understanding by processing our experiences through whatever filters we have.

Our spirit is where God connects to us. It's the immediately redeemed part of us at the moment of our salvation. When God speaks to us, He speaks to our spirit, not our soul. Our spirit is not limited by our life experiences. Our spirit is the part of us that truly and really knows God. It's not limited by human knowledge or understanding.

When we prophesy to someone, we do it out of our spirit that is connected to the Holy Spirit, not out of our soul. We have seen people prophesy out of their soul. What does that look like? It's when someone shares what they think, their thoughts, their concepts, and their ideas while calling it prophecy. What they "prophesy" is coming out of what they understand rather from God's Spirit. In doing so, they may share some good wisdom, but it's not prophecy.

True biblical prophecy is independent of our soul. It comes from our spirit connecting to God's Spirit. In this process we are receiving the mind of Christ for what we are prophesying about. It is no longer our thoughts but God's. This does not mean your soul is turned off and God has taken over your body. It means what you're releasing is not coming from your soul. Your soul submits to the Holy Spirit flowing through your spirit.

We still need our souls, it's what makes us humans and connects us to people. While ministering, we should not be led by it. However, we may pull knowledge from our soul to be able to communicate the spiritual intent of God, as discussed in Chapter 4. For example, you might know that God wants to release His love to whom you're prophesying. Your example to convey that message could be, "God wants to hold you like a mom or dad would hold their newborn baby. He is looking at you as proud as a new parent holds and sees their baby for the first time."

You understand what that concept is like from your soul based on what you have experienced. You may be a parent and have had that experience, or you have seen others have that experience. My soul knows and understands that concept. However, I'm using that language to convey the intent of God, that I received in my spirit from the Holy Spirit. My soul experiences give me language to convert Holy Spirit revelation so someone else can receive the heart and intent of God.

It's the union of the Holy Spirit that is sharing with us the mind, will, emotions, and intent of God. It's not our thoughts or opinions. They are God's thoughts and opinions. When we are prophesying, we have to separate our thoughts from God's thoughts.

Having the Mind of Christ

First Corinthians 2:16 says, *"For who has understood the mind of the Lord so as to instruct him?' But we have the mind of Christ."* We are prophesying from the mind of Christ. It's us taking a peek into the mind of Christ for the person to whom we are prophesying. It is separate from our natural mind.

Romans 12:2 says, *"Do not be conformed to this world, but be transformed by the renewal of your mind...."* Our mind must become His mind, and our thoughts must become His thoughts when we prophesy. This is an act of laying down yourself and what you think to receive what God thinks. His thoughts are higher than our thoughts and His ways higher than ours (Isaiah 55:9). We must always submit to His thoughts when prophesying to someone.

What You Believe Can Hinder or Help the Prophetic Flow

Your personal understanding and beliefs can hinder or help your prophetic flow. There are people who believe certain things about God that are not truly accurate.

We know one particular minister who comes from a more tradition denominational background. He believes the only way to serve God is in full-time pulpit ministry. He does not have the revelation about believers being called to the marketplace. He spends a lot of time praying for his son to come back to God. The funny thing is that his son is an on-fire Christian. He works in the marketplace and is making a powerful impact for the Kingdom.

However, the dad can't see his son's ministry because of his current theological understanding. God had called the son to the marketplace. That young man is doing exactly what God has called him to do. However, the father would never release a prophetic word about doing the will of God in the marketplace, because he does not believe that's God's will.

It's hard to prophesy beyond your theology. Make sure you stay connected to ministries that are teaching the present truth and now revelation of God. This will keep you open to receive the fullness of what God wants to release to whomever you're ministering.

Gifts Are Given for the Benefit of Others

The gifts of the Spirit are not given for your own benefit. They are given for the purpose of serving someone else. We are called to love people and serve them with what God has given us. The prophetic gift is to reveal God's heart to someone through edification, exhortation, and comfort.

I advise not to prophesy over yourself and make life decisions based on the word you gave yourself. There's really no need to prophesy over yourself at all. Instead, just talk to God about your situation and receive His heart. Always seek counsel from the spiritual authority in your life. You could also be filtering that word to yourself through your own soul. Proverbs 11:14 says, *"Where there is no guidance, a people falls, but in an abundance of counselors there is safety."* Just because you hear from God does not mean you have the full picture about yourself or others. It's always good to submit your revelation to the counsel of others to get a better picture and keep you safe. Submitting will produce good fruit in your life.

Gifts Versus Fruit

Spiritual gifts are given, but spiritual fruit is grown. Every Spirit-filled believer can flow in the prophetic. However, using the gift does not mean you have a godly character or maturity in the things of God.

In our church, we have eight-year-olds who prophesy. The gift has been activated in them. This does not mean they are mature. They may still misbehave and do things that they're not supposed to do. They are still learning and growing in maturity, in godly character and self-control. The same is true for all of us. We are still growing in the fruit of godly character and maturity.

The fruits of the Spirit are found in Galatians 5:22-23, which says, *"But the fruit of the Spirit is love, joy, peace, patience, kindness, goodness, faithfulness, gentleness, self-control; against such things there is no law."* These are the characteristics of Jesus. In other words, this is how He behaves and expects us to behave. They are called fruit because they have to be grown. It's not a gift, you don't just automatically behave like this.

Just because a believer is functioning in the gifts does not mean everything in his or her life is in right alignment. It means they have faith to operate in the gift. The fruit of the Holy Spirit comes when you learn to submit to the working of the Holy Spirit in your life. It's a day-by-day process of learning and growing. It's like a natural fruit tree. If the tree does not have fruit on it, you may not know what kind of fruit tree it is if you're not familiar with fruit trees. But when it has fruit on it, you know what kind of tree it is. The fruit of the Spirit comes over time as you let the Holy Spirt work in your life through pruning, watering, fertilizing, adding sun and growing you. Then the fruit is grown in your life. The fruit is just as important as the gift. It may even be more important. They are both expressions of Jesus.

Gifts Versus Leadership

Using the gifts of the Spirit in a powerful and mighty way does not qualify us for leadership. We should not promote or place people in places of authority based on gifting only. We need people with right character in places of leadership. Right character and gifting should be in balance in their lives. Human thinking says place the person with the most gifting and charisma in leadership, they are the greatest among us—but that's not how God chooses leaders.

In First Samuel we see God first choose Saul to be king of Israel, because that is who the people thought looked like a good leader. However, Saul's character was not the best. God's heart was for David to lead, because David was a man after God's own heart (Acts 13:22). In Acts 13:36 we see that David's heart was to serve the purpose of God in his generation. Even when David sinned, he was quick to repent; see Psalm 51. The heart to serve, like David had, is needed for leadership. Gifts can be activated and anyone can be taught to prophesy, but a heart to serve and maturity are what make truly great leaders.

Maturity Versus Spirituality

Someone can be very spiritual but not mature. Spiritual means you are aware and open to the spirit world. A spiritual person may hear God well. They may use the gifts of the Spirit in an amazing way. However, doing all this does not mean you are mature in God. Maturity in God is being governed by the character, nature, and ways of Christ. It is demonstrating the fruit of the Spirit.

Maturity means you are submitted to God in your soul and your behavior. Maturity is being governed by the principles as much as the presence of God. We have known people who could move in a powerful way in the gifts of the Spirit. They had such accurate words of knowledge. They seemed spiritual. However, they were mean in their interaction with people. They were verbally abusive, controlling, and angry. They were spiritual but not mature. God wants both in all of us.

The Fruit of Prophecy

The fruit of prophecy will produce clarity and direction. It will give you a knowing of what God wants to do in your life. You may not have all the understanding of every detail; however, it can be a huge guiding force leading you forward in vision and God's purpose for you. Knowing what God has called you to do will create a sense of security in your heart and soul. It will draw you closer to the Lord and connect you to Him.

God purposefully does not give you all the answers in a prophetic word. He will give you ideas and direction, but it's through your personal relationship with Him that you will receive the details. Prophecy is not to replace hearing God's voice for yourself. Above any of the gifts, the greatest and most powerful demonstration will come out of your own heart connection to Him. Prophecy aids our relationship with God, it does not replace it.

The prophetic word is also a catalyst. It will start and create the process for that prophetic word to be activated and established in a person's life. For example, you may get a word about writing a book. Before you got that word, maybe you had no desire to write a book. Once you received that word, you now have a passion to write a book. The prophetic word was a catalyst to birth the desire from God to write a book.

Activation

Pray in the Spirit for one hour. This will help you connect your spirit to God's Spirit. Your mind may wander and all kinds of thoughts will go through your head. This way you will see the separation of soul and spirit. Your spirit is praying but your soul and mind are all over the place.

Chapter 9

PROTOCOLS IN PROPHECY

Prophecy is a tool that can be used for good when done rightly. But the same tool can be used for harm, whether by ignorance or by intent. Protocols are wisdom to guide us in using these gifts the way God intends, for the best of the person receiving. Protocols include how to manage negative words, things not to prophesy while still a beginner, how to be a New Testament prophet (not Old Testament), what your responsibility is with what you hear from God, and principles of wisdom.

How to Manage a Negative Word

We were once ministering at a conference where they assigned someone to help us at the event. That is a normal practice in most conference cultures. We always like to connect and get to know the person assigned to assist us. However, this time it was very hard to connect with the guy. He would not get too close to us. He did not make eye contact very much and stood at a distance. We barely could corner him into a hug or a kind interaction. He did his job effectively, offering us beverages, carrying boxes, and generally serving us in a kind way. He just wouldn't get close.

Finally, on the last day, he told us why. He said one time at his church, a prophet came and called him out of the crowd along with the guy he was sitting beside. The prophet said in front of the whole church, "You two are in a homosexual relationship." The prophet began to tell him how horrible of a person he was for being gay. The word was accurate about his relationship with the man next to him. However, it did not draw him back to the Lord. It brought shame on him. It brought the issue to the surface in a devastating way rather than a way that could provide safety for healing and restoration. The Bible says it's the kindness of God that leads us to repentance. This man left the church for many years and completely rebelled against God.

By the time we met him, he had come back to the Lord and turned away from his previous lifestyle. But he was still carrying some shame and pain from the experience. He had made up in his mind that he would never attend a church or event where there would be prophets. He was terrified when his pastor said he was going to host a prophetic conference. He wanted no part of it.

Then his pastor asked him to assist us, the prophets who were coming to speak. He said, "I was avoiding you two because I know you're prophets, and I thought you were going to be harsh. But then I watched you minster to all these people with such love, gentleness, and hope to everyone." He explained that he now trusted us, and he asked us to minister to him before leaving. We were able to prophesy and pray with him to let go of the shame. We saw him fully transform, and today he is married and in ministry.

The prophetic is a very powerful tool, but we must use it in the right way to heal people and not to hurt them. Never use the prophetic to embarrass someone. Use it to empower people toward God and toward their destiny.

While receiving a prophetic word for someone from the Lord, you may pick up on some negativity. You many sense sin, something demonic, bad choices the person is making. It can be any number of negative things. God may be showing you the negative so you have a better understanding of what's going on. Anything God reveals is not to hurt or shame someone. We all have issues. Welcome to the human race. The key is to not stay in the negative but get to the positive. Whatever negative thing God reveals, it's because He desires to bring the situation into a positive one.

For example, if you sense that someone has an anger problem, you may not want to say, "God says you have an anger problem." The Lord is showing you what the current situation is, but that's not His end result. His end result is the opposite of anger for that person. What is the opposite of anger? Love, gentleness, self-control, happiness. The opposite of any negative situation is God's truest desire for the situation. God is never declaring the negative over someone's life. What you could say instead is, "God says He is giving you His love, causing you to be gentle, filling your heart with joy...." That's a better way to handle what was a seemingly negative word.

You can pray with someone about a negative area, but avoid prophesying negativity to someone. The prophetic word is to edify, exhort, and comfort. There is not much edifying or comfort in telling someone they have an anger problem. You edify, exhort, and comfort by telling the person the promise of where God wants to take them. The promise is freedom from an anger problem to joy, happiness, love, and self-control.

People usually know they have an anger problem. What they don't know is that there is hope that they can change. When you release the word of hope—the promise from God of who they are made to be—it gives them faith that God can set them free. The prophetic then becomes a key that can unlock them from the negative thing they are tied to.

Here's another example. Let's say you feel someone has a spirt of poverty. A harsh way to prophesy about it: "The Lord is showing me you have a spirit of poverty, you're poor, you can't pay your bills, you haven't had any nice clothes in years, and your car is not reliable. Your life really is a mess. Bless your heart! Amen."

A more productive way to prophesy about it: "The Lord is showing me that it is time for you to prosper, to have more than enough money to pay your bills and meet your needs. It's time for you to have some things that you can buy brand-new, that is a blessing to your heart. God is setting you free from the poverty that has come against you. God wants to move you into prosperity."

Do you see the difference? We hit all the same issues, but we ministered it in a way that produces the life of the Holy Spirit. It does not give the enemy words that he can use later to shame them and beat them up. Most people know their problems. What they need to know from the prophetic gift is God's promises and heart for them about it.

As a prophetic voice, our job is to connect people to the heart of God. We are to build a bridge from where people are to where God is and where He wants to take them. The prophecy breaks down walls in the heart and connects to the heart of God. If our prophetic ministry pushes someone away from God, it might not be being done with the best wisdom. We need wisdom and revelation. Revelation in the example is that a person has a spirit of poverty, the wisdom is saying it in a way they can receive the word and get free.

God's voice is restorative and redemptive. He is seeking to connect us to His heart in a greater way. When He speaks, it's to draw us closer.

If you're a leader and there is sin in the life of someone you're overseeing, then as a leader you can address it and walk them through a process of healing in love and privacy. The heart of God is always to heal—not to hurt. Calling out someone's sin publicly, in many cases, sets someone up to be hurt and possibly walk away from God.

Our primary function when we prophesy is to release prophetic words that edify, exhort, and comfort. We reveal and release the heart of God to people. The prophetic word should reveal destiny, potential, purpose, identity, etc. The prophetic word should be empowering people to be freed from their sin, bondage, or limitation.

Five Areas Beginners Should Avoid

As we train people around the world in the prophetic, there are five areas we encourage beginners to avoid. We recommend these areas for more seasoned ministers and fivefold ministers to manage. Someone with more prophetic ministry experience will have the wisdom, maturity, and understanding of how to minister in these areas so that they don't cause confusion and emotional angst. They can also counsel and walk someone through these areas to get the healthiest and best results.

Avoiding these five areas as a beginner will protect you and the person you are ministering to, keeping everyone safe and in a healthy, prophetic atmosphere. There is nothing more discouraging as a beginner than feeling like you made a big mistake. Avoiding these areas will help you avoid some casualties of learning and growing. The five areas are marriage, babies, death, geographical move, and the fivefold calling. Let's look at each one in more detail.

1. **Marriage:** It is best to avoid ministering to people about who they are specifically supposed to marry—even if you feel that you know two people are supposed to get married. We recommend praying with them about it if you have a close enough relationship with them to do so. If you don't, pray for them from a distance. When two people get married, they will be the ones who live out their covenant, not you and not even God.

2. **Babies:** Until you're well-seasoned in prophetic ministry, we recommend avoiding prophesying the date a child will be born, genders, or number of children. We suggest instead saying something like, "Let me agree with you in prayer about this." This takes the pressure off you and them, and gives you the chance to practice without making such a strong statement while you're learning.

3. **Death:** This is a very sensitive subject. You may sense that it's someone's time to pass away. If so, then you have a responsibility to pray. First, pray for the person's life to be extended if God wills it. Then pray and intercede for the family. Telling someone that he or she is going to die can create a lot of fear and panic. Also, if it's not really

God's time, you don't want to partner with a spirit of death.

4.   **Geographical Move:** We advise people not to
prophesy to someone to move geographically to
a new location. There is so much tied into someone's life when it comes to moving—job, family,
local church, and ultimately the person's destiny
are all connected to where they live. Your word
may be true, but the timing might not be the
present. Just pray about it and the timing of the
Lord for that person. Pray that God will give him
or her clarity in their own spirits about the timing to move. You can also prophesy to the issue
in a less direct way, so the word is still released as
confirmation if the person is already considering
it. An example of this is prophesying something
like, "God is opening the doors of transition in
your life."

5.   **Fivefold Calling:** We recommend not saying
to someone, "You're an apostle, prophet, pastor, teacher, evangelist." It would be better to say,
"You're called to be an apostle, prophet, pastor,
teacher, evangelist." This lets the person know he
or she may be called to that but have to wait on
God's timing and process. This way the person
doesn't quit his or her job, print business cards
with the fivefold title on it, and move out of
God's timing.

We know in part and we prophesy in part. Even if you're totally sure about the sensing you have about marriage, babies, death, geographical moves, and fivefold callings, these life-altering matters must be handled with maturity and wisdom. That's why we recommend beginners avoid these areas as they are starting out. And prophecy is in part, so most of all, the timing may still not be what we think it is.

If the Lord is strongly leading you to minster in one of these areas, of course, above all, we encourage you to obey God. There are ways to prophetically minister in these areas that can make it easier and safer. You can always pray the prophetic word for them or minister to them indirectly, where they can still receive what they need without us limiting it.

The following are some examples of how you can indirectly minister these areas:

- **Babies:** "The Lord wants to give you the godly desires of your heart and fulfill the promise you've long waited for."

- **Marriage:** "God is connecting your heart with destiny relationships. You're going to find deep fulfillment in the partnerships He is building in your life."

- **Death:** Pray for them to accomplish everything God has called them to do.

- **Geographical Moves:** "The Lord is connecting you to regions where you will have influence and walk in your purpose in a greater way."

- **Fivefold Calling:** "God has given you an anointing to demonstrate His heart of fathering" (pastoral)… or "…to break down His word with accuracy" (teacher)…, etc.

Yes, these examples seem vague, at least to the outsider. But to the people who have deep longings in their hearts, they know God is promising them a baby! To those who have been considering a job that would relocate them to a new city, they know God is opening that region to them for their purpose to be fulfilled. Remember, revelation breeds revelation. The Holy Spirit will further expound on the word you give in that person's spirit.

Following these guidelines while you practice will help you stay safe and keep others safe in the culture of prophetic ministry. We don't have to prophesy and share everything we sense. Some words you receive should just be prayed about and not released. God may be showing you something because He loves you and wants to share His heart with you.

New Testament Versus Old Testament Prophets

There is a difference between Old and New Testament prophets. Their purpose and how they function are different.

In the Old Testament, the Spirit of God would come on the prophets and they would release the word of the Lord. For example, Ezekiel 11:5 (NIV) says:

> Then the **Spirit of the Lord came on me**, and he told me to say: "This is what the Lord says: 'That is what you are saying, you leaders in Israel, but I know what is going through your mind.'"

In the New Testament, the Spirit of God does not come on them but from inside them. Romans 8:9 (NIV) says:

> You, however, are not in the realm of the flesh but are in the realm of the Spirit, if indeed the **Spirit of God lives in you**. And if anyone does not have the Spirit of Christ, they do not belong to Christ.

During Old Testament times, God did not speak directly to His people. He spoke only through prophets. There was a distance between the people and God. The nation was given instructions on what to do from prophets. The function of the Old Testament prophets was to point people to the law to reveal their need for a savior. They were leading and pointing to Jesus, the promised Messiah.

> But now the righteousness of God has been manifested apart from the law, although the Law and the Prophets bear witness to it—the righteousness of God through faith in Jesus Christ for all who believe. For there is no distinction (Romans 3:21-22).

The New Testament prophets' function is to equip the body of Christ. This is revealed to us in Ephesians 4:12, which says "to equip the saints for the work of ministry, for building up the body of Christ." Prophets are gifts from Jesus to the body of Christ. They activate believers to hear God, and reveal their purpose and place in the body.

> For the body does not consist of one member but of many. If the foot should say, "Because I am not a hand, I do not belong to the body," that would not make it any less a part of the body (1 Corinthians 12:14-15).

We are all parts of the body and all have a role to play in the body for it to become mature and fully functional. The New Testament prophets help to accomplish this. They help prepare the body of Christ for the return of Jesus.

Jermaine Here

Rebecca and I were ministering at a church in Texas that we had been to before, this was our second time. A few days before we arrived, the leader of the event found a recording of a prophetic word she had received about two years earlier. It was a word I gave her when she had visited CI for prophetic training. That was the first time I had met her. She returned home and started a new ministry with the purpose of training people in the gifts of the Spirit.

That weekend she had invited Rebecca and me to activate people in the gifts of the Spirit. The prophetic word was literally describing, word for word, what she was now doing in her ministry two years later. It described exactly what we were there that weekend to minister on. I would never have guessed that I would have been a part of helping her fulfill the prophetic word I gave her two years before. Honestly, I didn't even remember giving the word.

When we prophesy to people, we rarely remember the prophetic word later. People will often talk to us about a prophecy they received as if we would remember, but rarely do we ever. It means more to the person than it means to us. For us, it's one of many prophecies we have released. We could never remember them all!

Deliverer, Not Enforcer

The good news is we're not supposed to remember them all. Have you ever had a mail carrier deliver a bill? You're supposed to do something with a bill when you receive it. You're supposed to pay it. If you don't pay it, the mail carrier might deliver you a late notice as well. You could get several late notices. Next, you may start getting debt collector letters.

Your mail carrier just keeps delivering them. But what if your mail carrier opened your mail? And what if he or she read the mail, and knew you weren't paying a bill that you were supposed to pay? First, that would be a gross violation of your privacy rights and federal law. It would be out of line for a mail carrier to try to hold you accountable for what you do with the mail he or she delivers. Second, it would be absurd for the mail carrier to intrude in someone else's life through the mail, especially when delivering hundreds even thousands of mail each day. Who could keep up with that?

When it comes to revelation, we are the mail carrier—we are not enforcers. If we step into the role of trying to enforce the word God gives someone through us, we enter into sin. This is the sin Jonah fell into. Jonah received prophetic revelation that God was going to do something specific. When that didn't happen, Jonah sulked. God rebuked Jonah for his narrow view. Jonah's purpose was not to make the prophecy come to pass. It was to deliver the revelation.

Dr. Bill Hamon teaches that personal prophecy is conditional. When we give the revelation to another person, it's between that person and God only. It's none of our business what someone does with a word the person receives. As prophetic ministers, we only know in part. We don't know every aspect of someone's life. So, we must not judge the person based on how we think he or she should be responding to the prophetic word.

Additional Wisdom

We've looked at some protocols for the way we minister. There is also wisdom about how to conduct ourselves to be the most effective as prophetic ministers. Let's look at some additional wisdom.

First, we should be in right alignment under a local church. If we're planted, our prophetic ministry will produce greater fruit. We also want to make sure our prophetic ministry is under a spiritual covering. We are all human and can miss it sometimes. Being under authority can help us stay healthy in the prophetic ministry, even if we make a mistake. This helps protect us and helps us grow.

Second, it's good to find out the beliefs and protocol of the church you attend concerning prophetic ministry. It's wise to know what they believe and how they expect prophetic ministry to be done in their church culture. Many churches accept the prophetic when it's done in a way their church culture is set up to receive it. Prophetic ministry is most effective when it is received. If they can't receive it, then it will not take root and bear fruit.

Our job as prophetic ministers is to create the best setting for people to receive what God has for them. We're not responsible if they receive it or not. We're just responsible to create the best atmosphere for them to be open to receive it.

Third, when we give the word, it's better not to counsel them about the word. If we start going in to counsel about the prophetic word we gave them, we might not have the clearest interpretation. We gave the word, that was our only job. Let them get counsel from their own spiritual covering. The Holy Spirit is the One who interprets the word, not us. Most of our prophetic words did not come to pass the way we thought they would. Neither will theirs. Neither will the words you give.

We should not interpret the prophetic words that we give and receive based on what we think or feel. The word comes from God. He knows what He has in mind when He speaks a word. We must always go back to God to get the right interpretation. It is the Spirit of God who brings illumination and understanding to the word.

We want the prophetic ministry that the Holy Spirit releases through us to be as impactful and effective as possible. We think that's what you want too. There are principles we can practice that will help set you up for the most success. We want to make sure we create healthy and proper prophetic culture. The prophetic can be strange enough, we don't need any reason to make it appear stranger. Our goal is to help people receive God's heart through the prophetic minister, not to be either impressed or repelled by it. Following healthy protocols will bring about the greatest return of godly fruit from your prophetic ministry.

Chapter 10

THE LANGUAGE OF PROPHECY

The Skill You Can Develop

Believers can train themselves to hear God's voice extensively, in detail, for any person or circumstance, at any time. So how do we do it?

Remember when you read about the theater of the mind in Chapter 4? God rarely gives us exact words to say to someone. Instead, He gives us meaning. The amazing thing is that revelation breeds revelation. One piece of revelation can quickly multiply into more, especially when we engage with it and pull on it, like you pull on a piece of string in your clothing. One piece of meaning that God gives to us is our invitation to more revelation.

> *The word of the Lord came to me: "What do you see, Jeremiah?"*
>
> *"I see the branch of an almond tree," I replied.*
>
> *The Lord said to me, "You have seen correctly, for I am watching to see that my word is fulfilled."*
>
> *The word of the Lord came to me again: "What do you see?"*
>
> *"I see a pot that is boiling," I answered. "It is tilting toward us from the north."*
>
> *The Lord said to me, "From the north disaster will be poured out on all who live in the land. I am about to summon all the peoples of the northern kingdoms," declares the Lord... (Jeremiah 1:11-15 NIV).*

God shows Jeremiah the branch of an almond tree. Then Jeremiah engages with that revelation when God asks him what he sees. Then God shows him more. God then shows him a pot boiling. Jeremiah engaging with the first revelation led him to the next piece of revelation.

Prophet Bill Lackie, who has trained hundreds of prophets at Christian International for nearly three decades, describes how to receive more detail and depth of revelation. He calls it "picking the leaves off the tree." In this analogy, any piece of revelation is like a tree trunk. Once you see the trunk, you can follow it to any branch you choose. Once you choose a branch, you can follow it to a stem. Once you choose a stem, you can see each leaf on that little stem. And then there's three leaves on the next stem. And there are more than 100 stems on that branch. And maybe there's seven branches on that tree.

The revelation from God is always available. The skill needed is the ability to follow the branches to the stems and the stems to the leaves, and repeat.

Jermaine Here

I remember one of my first times as a prophetic team member at our church. The teams were structured so that someone more advanced was with a new person as a mentor and to train. I was the newbie. This particular time, I was prophesying and told a young man he was called to the business world. My team leader asked how? I said, "I see you're called to lead in the business world." What position are they called to in the business world? I said, "He is called to be CEO of a company." The team leader said, "Yes, good job." The team leader already had that word about the man being called to be a CEO. I was being taught and trained to follow the branches and press in for more revelation and details. As I was asked the question, God immediately showed me the answers to the question. I learned in that moment to ask the Holy Spirit questions on each piece of revelation He shows me and then He will release the details. God is not just throwing information out there—He gives it to seekers.

Another thing that increases revelation is staying with the same topic, but elaborating more thoroughly. We find some of the most impactful prophecies we have ever given were only about a single topic. The longer we stayed on that one topic, the more God gave us deeper revelation, accurate details, and an increased anointing.

This works because the longer you talk about something, the more you engage in it, and the more the person receiving engages in it. As you tell the story of what God is saying to the person, the person connects with his or her heart in a greater way. That connection is priceless. At the same time, as you use more words to share this one thing God is saying, you have to press in to God for more. You'll receive more from Him to give because you pressed past the easy part.

When it comes to revelation, don't let yourself think, *That's all I got* about anything God shows you. The Bible says it's the glory of God to conceal a matter, and the honor of kings to search it out. When God gives you one piece of revelation, consider it an invitation to search out the vast supernatural reality hidden behind that one word.

Learn as You Go

Learn to ask questions as you go. If you normally get one word, press yourself for one sentence. After you normally receive one sentence, press yourself for a paragraph. Always put a demand on the gift of prophecy inside of you.

Practice is not just for hobbies. Many preachers take public-speaking courses, practice making outlines, practice their jokes, punchlines, and deliveries. In fact, every field practices their craft. You may not consider yourself a prophet, but you are called to prophesy, so practice.

At Christian International, where we have trained as prophets since 2005, we have done this kind of practice more times than we can ever count. But you don't have to dedicate hours at a time or be in a group of other prophetic people. You can do this kind of practice during your devotion time with the Lord, while driving in your car, or any time.

Another way to look at it is like you're walking around the rooms of a house. When you walk inside the house, what do you do at the very beginning? You basically take a quick assessment of everything that's there. You might see that there is a living room, a kitchen, a laundry room, and assume there is one bedroom or more.

After you do that, you may feel like you have a pretty good assessment of what's inside the house. You basically know what is there at a glance. That's similar to how most of us initially receive a prophetic revelation from God. We sort of see everything that is there and think we get it. But the truth is, there's so much more beneath what we see that can be explored more thoroughly if we take the time.

So when you enter that house or apartment, first take an assessment of everything that's there. But then take the time to go into each room individually. Once you open the door of a room, look around and notice the major aspects first and then if you want to take more time you can notice the minor details. So, you might open the door and see that there is a bed and a window. But if you look closer, you would see papers on a desk. And if you look even closer, you might see the topics that are written on the paper. The depth of detail available is almost endless. The question is whether you will take the time to explore and how deep you want to go in that exploration.

So this is what it's like when we prophesy. We can take the revelation as deep as we want. That's how I may do it when I prophesy. Often God will give us five areas quickly that we can see within a short window of time. We just quickly take inventory of those areas in our mind, just like looking into a home.

So, I take a quick inventory: there's an office, bathroom, guest bedroom, kitchen, and living room. Now as I prophesy, I will go deeper into each of those topics remembering that there are more topics to cover next—depending on any time restraints.

This is a process of "spiritual multitasking." The first time we heard about this, it seemed a little overwhelming, but it actually took very little time to get the hang of it. It takes more effort to explain it than it actually does to do it. It may seem complicated right now, but if you train yourself intentionally just a couple of times to do this, you'll find you do it naturally anytime revelation comes.

Meaning Not Always Known

I remember giving a word to someone and saying, "God is healing your heart of the loss and the season of grieving that you have just gone through is coming to an end." In my mind I thought maybe the person had a death in the family. Then I find out the person just moved to the area. However, it felt like a death process to the person and he was grieving. The word did not mean to the person what I thought it could possibly mean.

Most of the prophecies we have given, once a person explained to us what it meant, turned out to be different from what it sounded like to us.

When we receive revelation for another person, we may feel like we know what it means, but honestly, we don't. Scripture says we know in part and we prophesy in part,[1] and that never changes, no matter how advanced we become in our prophetic gifts.

It's dangerous to think we fully know what a prophetic word means for another person. We do well to deliver the word as we receive it, asking questions and expanding, but never assuming the meaning. However, when we think we know what it means, such as what it would mean to us, or what we may already know about the person, we cross over from prophecy to giving counsel in our own knowledge. Giving counsel might not be bad, but doing it in the name of God when it is actually our assumption is risky business.

There's never a need to explain the revelation beyond what we receive. While we can always ask God for more detail, we should never try in our own minds to create the detail or explanation.

Prophetic Terminology

Another reason we don't know what a prophecy really means is that revelation is sometimes apart from time and different from the current manifest reality. Something we see in the spirit could look so immediate and real, yet be decades away in the natural realm. Remember that in eternity there is no time, and eternity is where God has birthed our destinies.

So let's talk a little about prophetic terminology. Dr. Bill Hamon covers this extensively in his book *Prophets and Personal Prophecy*. We strongly encourage you to read that book for a strong biblical understanding of the personal prophecies you receive! We mention a couple small points here, which we learned from him.

The language of revelation is rarely as literal and straightforward as our language. When God refers to time, it's not equal to our timetable. The following is a breakdown from Dr. Bill Hamon's book *Prophets and Personal Prophecy,* cited on page 123:

- "Immediately" means from one day to three years.

- "Very soon" means one to ten years.

- "Now or this day" means one to forty years.

- "I will" without a definite time designation means God will act sometime in the person's life if the person is obedient.

- "Quickly" was the term Jesus used to describe the time of His soon return—almost 2,000 years ago. "Behold, I come quickly."

Controlling the Delivery

We have control over how we deliver the prophetic word. Another thing to remember is that we always have a choice in how we deliver the revelations. The Scripture says that the gift of prophecy is subject to the prophet. This means that we are never out of control in how we minister. We can never say that God made us minister a certain way, or that He made us prophesy through this certain word, or that anything else was beyond our control.

Interestingly enough, most of what revelation we get from God we don't actually share. This is because, as you can imagine, the more revelation you learn to receive, it's not even possible to really share it all. But that's not really the main reason why we don't share all of it. We have found, as our mentor prophet Bill Lackie says, most revelation is more useful for prayer than it is for sharing. And if we can learn to be good stewards of the revelation and share and pray that through for God, then we will be trusted even further with the things He wants to share. So just as we can choose our words, we can also choose to refrain from sharing certain things or not to share all, depending on the greatest benefit.

ENDNOTE

1. 1 Corinthians 13:9-12.

Chapter 11

PRACTICING MORE

Over a decade ago, when both of us started training in the prophetic, we were not as confident about our ability to hear God as we are today. We were probably just as accurate, and just as effective, but we didn't quite know that we knew how to prophesy.

Knowing comes with time. Confidence comes with time. So what do you do in the meantime? Do you prophesy when you are not confident, and you don't know for sure if you're hearing God? The answer is a simple yes—in faith, in Christ, you just do it.

Let's ask some tough questions. How do you know that what you were thinking is from God? It could've just been your imagination, right? Well, not exactly. It's easy to know when you're hearing from God. You know you're hearing from God the same way you know you're saved—by faith! You can't prove you're saved. You might not know what it feels like to feel saved. The way you know you're saved is if you believe the Word of God, that if you believe in your heart and confess with your mouth that Jesus is Lord, and repent from your sins—then you know you will be saved, by faith.

You know you're saved by faith, and you know you're hearing God by faith. You believe the Scriptures that you've read throughout this book, that God wants to speak to you, and that you can hear His voice. You believe the Scripture that says if you asked for bread, He will not give you a stone.[1] So you believe in your heart, and then you act in faith. We call this activating.

When we ask God to speak to us, He does. I heard some-one say our first thought is usually God; the second thought is us talking ourselves out of the fact it's God. We are designed to hear God. So we do. The enemy is the one that brings in doubt. When the enemy speaks, we sometimes believe him faster than we believe God. When God speaks, we start to question and ask God for multiple confirmations. Trust that you hear from God.

Activating in Raw Faith

Dr. Bill Hamon teaches activating as a foundational practice. In fact, he's the one who coined the phrase more than 50 years ago. Activating simply means acting on what you believe. When you were saved, most likely someone told you about God, or about salvation. Most likely you learned that if you pray a prayer, or repent for your sins, or ask Jesus into your heart, you'll be saved. So you did! You heard that message, you believed, and then you acted. The action you took is opening your mouth, or quietly in your head, to speak according to what you now believe. The action was the prayer. Once you prayed, you were saved! It was that simple. The way you knew you were saved was because you believed you were.

Prophecy, and all the gifts of the Spirit, work exactly like salvation. First you hear the Scripture or promise from God, then you believe it, then you act on it. The action is when you choose to deliver the revelation you received.

At Christian International, when we train people to acti-vate, they're almost all nervous—every time! People get a little nervous about the idea of speaking for God, especially if they haven't done it before or if they're feeling put on the spot in the moment. So we tell them, "If you didn't receive anything, share what you would have shared if you had received some-thing." Usually that gets a pretty good laugh, but it's not just a joke. It's true!

If you did get something from God, you would share it con-fidently because you know it was from God. And we believe that if you asked God to speak to you, just like if you ask Him for bread, that He won't be silent, just like He wouldn't give you a stone rather than bread. So, if you ask God to speak to you, then the only faith-filled response afterward is to step out in boldness and share what you think might be from God. Acting in faith is the way to go forward and build your faith and your gifts.

We don't need to "feel" anything to prophecy. You might, you might not. We are prophesying by submitting and yielding our spirit to God. It's not an emotional thing. True faith actu-ally has no emotion. Emotions are soul based. True and pure faith is just believing what God says no matter how you feel. It's faith in God. Submitting and yielding our spirit to Him honors God more than just believing Him at His word.

Reason of Use

Raw faith is almost always the first step, but it's not the only part of the equation. The more often you use your faith, *"by reason of use"* as the Scripture says,[2] the more comfortable you will get with what God's voice sounds like to you and how to discern when you are hearing Him. It will always require faith, but you will grow more and more familiar with what that voice sounds like and how to operate in faith.

In that regard, we're almost always nervous when we proph-esy. We never think to ourselves, *I've got this in the bag!* And we approach prophecy with humility, humbling ourselves before God and before the person who we're going to bless. So the nervousness never completely disappears, and you never have a 100 percent guarantee, as if there's a fail-safe way to prophesy. If we did, we would start to do it apart from God.

The whole process works only with a relationship with God! It all works around your faith, and in intimacy with Him. Without both, what's the point anyway? So it's not like every time God is speaking to one of us, the other says, "My left toe tingles," so as to clue us that what we're hearing is God. That would be super handy, but it's just not the way it works.

The best way it works is by reason of use. It's simple repetition. The more you use the muscle, the more familiar you will be, the more comfortable you'll be, the more confident you will be, and the more you'll trust God and trust His voice in your spirit.

Stir it Up

The last aspect of knowing you're hearing from God is simply making the choice to stir up the gift. We talked so much already about how hearing God really is up to us, since He is constantly communicating. Paul told Timothy to *"stir up the gift of God which is in you"* by the laying on of hands.[3] That sentence clearly put responsibility on Timothy. Who is supposed to stir? Timothy! Who has the gift of God? Timothy! Sure, someone else activated it. Sure someone else laid hands on him. Someone else mentored him. Someone else taught and instructed him. Someone else even provoked him to stir up the gift. But at the end of the day, Timothy is the one who has to stir up his own gift.

"Stir up" doesn't mean stir up your emotions. It doesn't mean hype up yourself or talk yourself into it. It simply means to activate what is already inside you. Place a demand on the gift that is already there. Put an expectation on yourself to hear God. Once you think you're comfortable with the frequency or depth that you hear God, then put a greater expectation on yourself. You can never connect too much! There is always more in God.

So when Paul told Timothy to stir up the gift, he was saying take action by your will as your own choice, and provoke inside you the potential that is there. And the same responsibility that Timothy had to stir himself up is the responsibility we have to stir up the gift of God that's inside us today.

Raw faith, reason of use, and stirring up the gift of God inside us are ways we will expand and deepen the gift of prophecy that we have. Whether we've been prophesying our whole lives or we've just begun today, the same principles apply and will produce fruit in our lives.

Now we know that stirring it up is necessary, and that simply stepping out in faith even when we're not sure is necessary, and that we have to do it over and over until it becomes more natural to us.

So now that you know this, let's discover ways you can choose to stir up, step out in faith, and repeat the process to continually go deeper in your walk of the prophetic.

ENDNOTES

1. Matthew 7:9.
2. Hebrews 5:14 NKJV.
3. 2 Timothy 1:6 NKJV.

ACTIVATIONS

This section of the book is all about training and unlocking the prophetic in you. This is additional practical, hands-on activation time. This just means we're going to help you stir up the gift of prophecy in you. Like Paul told Timothy, as we mentioned earlier in Second Timothy 1:6-7 NKJV. stir up the gift of God in you. Timothy was responsible to do this. We are responsible to stir up the gifts of God in our lives. This section is all about you stirring up the gift of prophecy.

To hear and flow in the gift of prophecy, you have to shift out of your thoughts and into the thoughts and flow of God. The following activations will help you begin to do that. Just like any skill, you might not be an expert at it on your first try. You get better each time you practice.

So be kind to yourself and enjoy the process of learning and growing.

Here are three quick ways you can prepare yourself to hear from God—read God's Word, worship, pray in the Spirit. Let's look at each of these in more depth.

The first is read the Bible. Reading the Bible familiarizes you with the voice of God and how He speaks and communicates. Just like when you read an email or text from a close friend, as you read the email, you can hear the friend talking. You can hear how a certain phrase or word would be said by your friend.

Reading the Bible is the same way. It gets you in the flow of hearing how God sounds when He speaks, which gets you more comfortable with the flow of His voice. Not only will you understand how He speaks, you'll also catch His nature and His heart, which are the most important. If you're going to speak for God, you don't want to be a robot just repeating words from God. You want to share and release His heart also.

However, if you have had harsh and traumatic experiences in life that you are not healed from, it can cause you to have a negative filter. Which can affect how you view God and His Word. We encourage you to pray the following prayer to set a right foundation and perspective of God and His Word:

> *Father, I come before You and I submit myself to You. If there is any wrong perspective or foundation of who You are in my mind, I release it now in Jesus' name. I ask for a clear and accurate perspective of who You are and Your heart. In Jesus' name!*

The second way to prepare yourself to hear from God is worship. This is a great way of shifting from your mind to God's mind. When you worship, you begin to focus on the Lord. When you worship, it begins to create an atmosphere for His presence. God is everywhere all the time; however, when you worship, it is like turning on a faucet and causing more of His presence to increase in that moment. Worship is a great atmosphere to receive and release prophetic words from God.

The third preparation is praying in the Spirit. When you pray in the Spirit, immediately your spirit connects to the Spirit of God and opens a communication channel. This channel bypasses your mind and logical understanding and immediately causes you to tap into the Spirit of God. This is a great way to shift out of your mind and shift into the mind of God.

Practicing these three ways of preparation will help your prophetic gifting to sharpen and grow.

Before you start the following activations, let's take a few minutes and do these three steps. First, read one chapter of the Bible. Then listen to a worship song and spend a few minutes worshipping the Lord. Then spend a few minutes praying in the Spirit. Open your heart to the Lord and He will pour His heart into yours.

Taking these three actions has now postured you to receive from God. Now go ahead and do the following activations. You don't have to do them all in one sitting; you can take the next few weeks and go through each activation. If you have a friend who wants to work with you, that would be great.

God's design and heart for the use of any of the gifts of the Spirit is always to bless someone else and not to serve your own needs. All of these activations are focusing outward, on someone else. We are stepping out there by faith and asking God to use you to bless and minister to someone else.

As you step out in the activations. We want you to follow each little piece of revelation you receive. The more you engage and follow that revelation, you'll be surprised how much more will flow to and through you.

Start with activation number one and follow the activations in order. They build on each other and will help you grow with each activation you do. We encourage you to take the next few weeks and work through each of these activations.

Activation Exercises

1. Pick a friend in your mind. Now, pray and ask the Lord to show you one thing for your friend. You may receive the word by seeing a picture, getting a feeling, getting an inner knowing, a thought flash through your mind. Pay attention to how you receive the word from God.

   Now take out a piece of paper or your iPad, laptop, or whatever you prefer to write on. Write what you received from God as a prophetic word. For example, you might write: My sensing for this friend is that God is building up the person. And your prophetic word may sound like: The Lord is building you up and strengthening you in the Spirit. Your spiritual muscles are growing and increasing. You may feel some resistance and discomfort, but those feelings are actually your spiritual muscles growing.

2. Now we're going to do the exact same thing—except this time don't write the word down, just prophesy it out loud. You might feel strange, but this is to help you learn how to release a prophetic word.

   Use the same friend you picked for Activation 1. Now, pray and ask the Lord to show you one thing for your friend. You may receive the word by seeing a picture, having a feeling, sensing an inner knowing, and or a thought may flash through your mind. Pay attention to how you receive the word from God.

3. Pick a friend, in your mind. Then ask God to give you a Scripture for that person. Wait. The first Scripture that comes to you either through seeing, hearing, sensing, or knowing is the Scripture for your friend. Don't overthink it.

    Then pull out a prophetic word from the Scripture for the person. For example, this Scripture popped into your mind: *"The grace of our Lord Jesus Christ be with you"* from First Thessalonians 5:28 in the English Standard Version.

    Now I will demonstrate by prophesying this verse to you. "Reader, God says I'm with you, right now, you're not alone. I'm proud of your desire and your heart to draw closer to Me. I want you to know that I'm closer to you than you know. I'm in this moment with you right now. I'm pulling down walls and bringing a greater closeness between you and Me."

    Now I will show you what I did. The main thing I felt from that verse was that God is with you. I began to feel what God's heart from that verse was for you, the reader, and me also. Then I began to write the feelings I sensed from the Lord about being with us. Now you do the same for whomever you're going to write the word for.

    After you have written the word, if you're feeling bold, send them a text message of what you sense God is saying to them. You don't have to begin with, "The Lord says." You can just say "Hey so and so, I sensed this for you and wanted to share it." This will give room to share it in confidence, without the person thinking you're strange by saying, "God says…."

4.   Pick a friend or close family member. Now ask the Lord to show you one thing that you can pray about for this specific family member. You're not going to pick something that you know or you desire to pray about, you are going to pick what the Lord instructs you to pray about.

When you have that one thing in your mind, go ahead and call that family member and say, "Hey, I would like to pray for you." Then begin to pray for the person, pray for what the Lord showed you to pray. We call this prophetically praying. Only pray for what the Lord has shown you to pray for at this moment.

5.   There is someone specific I have in mind. You don't know who the person is. You're going to pray and ask the Lord to show you one thing for this person. You may receive the word by seeing a picture, having a feeling, sensing an inner knowing, and or a thought flashes through your mind.

Without knowing anything else, take about five minutes and write out a prophetic word for that person. Once you're finished, I will reveal who that person is.

To see who the prophetic word is for, go to the Answer Key on the last page in this Activations chapter. The answer is that the prophetic word is for person (C). Now read the word with person (C) in mind. See if you can see elements of the word that you know are true and apply to the person. You might not know every detail of that person's life, so you might not be able to verify everything you wrote down. But it helps to compare what you do know about the person.

6. Grab a piece of paper or type on your laptop or phone. At the top write the name of your city or town. Then write this for your first sentence: The Lord says to the region of _____. (Fill in the blank)

    Set a timer for three minutes and then pray in the spirit and think about the love that God has for the region. Receive His heart about your city or town. At the end of that three minutes, set the timer again, this time for ten minutes. During this time, add to that first sentence, write out a prophetic word for your region. Don't spend time thinking about it. Spend that next ten minutes writing down everything that is flowing through you. Try to write for the entire ten minutes.

    When you're done, read back through the word. See what the Holy Spirit caused to flow through you. It might be surprising what was said through you that you have no natural idea about.

    This activation will begin to unlock the prophetic flow inside you.

7.   We are going to repeat Activation 6. This time without paper. Pray in the spirit for three minutes. Then set a timer for five minutes. This time I want you to begin out loud to prophesy to your city or town. Speak the prophetic word out. Try to keep prophesying over your region for the entire five minutes. It might be hard at first, but push yourself. It will grow your prophetic gifting.

You can start with, "The Lord says to…." Then just let it flow. This will help build and increase your prophetic flow.

8.   Write the word HOPE at the top of a piece of paper or your screen. Now pick a friend on social media. Then write out a prophetic word to that person about hope. You can start the word like this, "The Lord says my hope is…." Then go into a flow about God's hope to the person. God has a lot to say about hope. Don't actually send this word to the person. This is just to give you someone to focus on to receive a word for.

9.   Again, write the word HOPE on the top of another piece of paper or another blank screen. This time set a timer for three minutes. Then write down as many descriptive or connective words that you can for "hope." For example, you may write words such as expectation, future, desire, joy, peace. Spend the full three minutes writing down every word that comes to your mind about hope.

At the end of the three minutes, circle the top ten words on the page. Now you're going to use those top ten words to write a prophetic word for the same person you wrote for Activation 8. Include all ten of those descriptive words in the prophetic word.

For example, I will use the words I used earlier to form the prophetic word: The Lord is renewing your hope and expanding your expectation for your future. He is unlocking new desires in you that will produce new joy and peace inside you.

You might notice there is now a greater depth to the prophetic flow to the same person. Vivid words help paint the picture more clearly. When you use descriptive words, you pull out the meaning more, and additional details will come.

10. Now I want you to prophesy to the same person again. This time I want you to release the word out loud. You can start with hope and let it flow. You should notice a more significant flow after completing the two previous activations.

11. We're going to repeat Activation 5 again—but this time it's for person (A). There is someone specific I have in mind. You don't know who the person is. You're going to pray and ask the Lord to show you one thing for this person. You may receive the word by seeing a picture, having a feeling, sensing an inner knowing, and or a thought flashes through your mind.

Without knowing anything else, take about five minutes and write out a prophetic word for that person. Once you're finished, I will reveal who that person is.

This word is for person (A) revealed in the Answer Key. Now read the word with person (A) in mind. See if you can see elements of the word that you know are true and apply to the person. You might not know every detail of that person's life, so you might not be able to verify everything you wrote down. But it helps to compare what you do know about the person.

12. Pick someone you know you will see tomorrow. For example, if you're going to work, pick a co-worker; if you're going to church, pick a church member; if it's your day off and you're running errands, it could be the person at the store that you see every week. If you're not leaving your house tomorrow, maybe a neighbor. Pray for the person and ask God what's one thing He is currently doing in the individual's life. It depends what your primary way of hearing from God is—you might see a picture, hear something, feel something, or just know something.

When you have received it, write it down, which helps you remember what the word is. Then— you guessed it—tomorrow when you see the person, share it with them.

You can say something like, "Last night I prayed for you, and this is what I feel God is doing in your life....

Some examples of what it may sound like:

- I feel like God is releasing peace in your home, to help you rest.

- I feel like some new opportunities are going to open up for you on your job.

- I feel like that whatever decision you're struggling with, God is giving you clarity.

These are just a few examples to give you a framework on how to shape what you receive from God for someone. Don't feel limited by these examples.

13. Pick a family member or a close friend who you know is currently in a place of transition in life. For example, looking for a job, just got a new position at work, moving, getting married, having a baby, has a child going off to college, buying a house, lost a job, starting a new business, starting a church or ministry, buying a car, etc.

Now I want you to ask the Lord what His heart is for the person who is in a place of transition. Not your opinion or thoughts on the matter, but God's heart. This is where you have to make sure your soulish mind is separated from receiving the heart and mind of God on the subject.

For example, we have a friend who is renovating her kitchen. My natural thoughts are, *That's exciting and fun, the kitchen will look so great.* This is my prophetic word for the transition: The Lord is shifting the atmosphere in your home and drawing you closer as a family. He is preparing your hearts to take on a more pastoral nature and to host people in your home to serve them, make them feel loved, inspired, and give them a sense of value and family.

You can call and share this word with your friend. You can say, "In the transition you're in, I feel like God is saying...."

Remember, you're not telling your friend what to do with her life, you're submitting the word to her to receive it for God. She will then have to walk that word out with God.

14. Pick someone to prophecy to. Then ask God to show you which part of His nature He is demonstrating in the person's life right now. An example is that God is the Healer, Provider, Comforter, Deliver, Good Shepard, King, Lord.

    The word may sound something like this: "The Lord is meeting your needs and bringing you ideas and opportunities for your needs to be met."

15. For this activation, follow each instruction carefully step by step.

    a.   I am going to lead you to prophesy over a specific individual.

b.　Right now, ask the Lord if this is a male or female. If the Lord says female, write "Daughter" at the top of your page or screen. If the Lord says male, write "Son" at the top.

c.　Now ask the Lord what He wants to say to this son or daughter. Wait on the Lord and receive what He is saying.

d.　Next, begin to write out that prophetic word to your son or daughter of God.

e.　Now read that word.

f.　Next, turn to the Answer Key to see who is this prophetic-word person (E).

The prophetic word was for *you.* Now read through that word and see the heart of God for you. See how much of the word you can relate to right away. Read and receive what God is saying to you. I love this activation because people really begin to see what they prophesied to themselves without realizing it was to themselves.

If you said son and you're a daughter, it does not mean the word is off. It means you might have been sensing this attribute or name of how God was communicating to you. For example, when we think female, we think caring, gentle, mothering, which could be the nature of what God wanted to communicate to you. He could be speaking to your nature of caring and gentleness in you. And vice versa, when you think of the nature of a male, you may think protector, provider, warrior. This could be the nature that's God is highlighting in you.

16. Pick a friend or coworker in your mind to whom you want to minister. This activation might seem a little strange, but it will help your prophetic gift to grow. Close your eyes and ask God to give you a picture as an inspiration for your prophetic word to the person.

    After you have received the picture, you will prophecy the elements of the picture to that person. Don't just tell the person, "I see a tree." You need to pull out a prophetic word from the tree.

    For example, if you saw a tree, the word could go something like this: "You are planted very deeply, you have deep connections to your family, church family, and friends. They have been the root systems in your life that have allowed you to grow as big and strong as you are. It has helped you to grow strong enough to now be a shade and a shelter for others but also is helping you to produce a great fruit from which others can come and receive and be blessed."

    The tree was the image that God used to give you concepts to communicate His heart to someone. When God gives you a picture, you can pull out all the meaning from it to create and communicate a full picture about what God is saying.

17. Pray and ask the Lord what He is saying to your social media audience. Receive whatever the Lord shows you. Then post it on your social media. Use a hashtag such as #DeepRoots.

18. Pick a friend. Now ask the Lord to give you a word about the person's future. The word could be about what he or she will be doing in the future, what will be accomplished, or who will be impacted.

    You can write, call, or text to share the word with them.

19. Pick a leader in the body of Christ. Just step out by faith and start to audibly prophesy over the person. Just start speaking out what you feel flowing up in you.

20. We're going to repeat Activation 5 again. But this time it's for person (D).

    Pray and ask the Lord to show you one thing for this person. You may receive the word by seeing a picture, having a feeling, sensing an inner knowing, or a thought may flash through your mind.

    Take about five minutes and write out a prophetic word for that person.

    This word is for person (D) in the Answer Key. Now read the word with person (D) in mind. See if you can see elements of the word that you know are true and apply to them. You might not know every detail of that person's life so you might not be able to verify everything you wrote down. But it helps to compare the things you do know about the person.

21. Ask a friend to work with you. Ask the friend to pick someone in his or her life that you don't know. The friend may or may not show you a picture. Then ask the Lord to give you a word for that person. Then begin to prophesy over that person in the presence of your friend. Let your friend listen to your prophecy. When you're done, ask your friend to tell you if what you said was true about that person. Since your friend knows the person and you don't, they may be able to confirm some things for you. This will help build your confidence.

22. Ask the Lord who in your life needs a word right now. Then ask Him for a word for that person. Then call the person and share the right now word with them.

23. Pray and ask the Lord to reveal is one thing that He is doing in your life in the next 24 hours. Write down whatever the Lord shows you. Then over the 24 hours, watch and see how the Lord confirms what He is doing in your life.

24. Now ask the Lord what He is saying about an area in which you have responsibility. For example,

your job, family, home, church, or any role you have in a specific area. It's always good to know God's heart for every area of your life. When you have a clear perspective of what God is doing and asking you to do, you can partner with Him in it in a greater way to see supernatural results.

25. We're going to repeat Activation 5 again. This time it's for person (B).

Pray and ask the Lord to show you one thing for this person. You may receive the word by seeing a picture, having a feeling, sensing an inner knowing, or a thought flashes through your mind.

Take about five minutes and write out a prophetic word for that person.

This word is for person (B) in the Answer Key. Now read the word with person (B) in mind. See if you can see elements of the word that you know are true and apply to the person. You might not know every detail of that person's life, so you might not be able to verify everything you wrote down. But it helps to compare the things you do know about the person.

26. Right where you are right now, begin to prophesy to the atmosphere of the room you are in. You might be at home, at work, at a coffee shop, on a plane, etc. What is God saying about where you currently are?

27. You can set your faith to prophesy in a certain area of someone's life. For example, you can set your faith to prophesy about someone's job, family, destiny, health, purpose, finances.

    Pick a friend or family member, then pick two areas from this list and ask the Lord for a word in those areas for your friend or family member. Then audibly begin prophesy to the person about those areas.

28. Look at a picture of a friend. Set a timer for ten minutes. Then prophesy out loud to the picture of that person for ten minutes. If you feel like you get stuck, use the descriptive words you read about in Activation 9. Stretch yourself and let your prophetic gifting grow.

29. We're going to repeat Activation 5 again—this time it's for person (F).

    Pray and ask the Lord to show you one thing for this person. You may receive the word by seeing a picture, having a feeling, sensing an inner knowing, or a thought may flash through your mind.

    Take about five minutes and write out a prophetic word for that person.

    This word is for person (F). Now read the word with person (F) in mind. See if you can see elements of the word that you know are true and apply to the person. You might not know every detail of that person's life so you might not be able to verify everything you wrote down. But it helps to compare the things you do know about the person.

Email a prophecy to us at info@jermaineandrebecca.com.

❀ ❀ ❀

Answer Key

(A) Current leader of your country

(B) Last person, you talked to either in person, by phone, or by text message

(C) Closest person in your life—spouse, friend, family member

(D) The first person you see when you open your social media feed

(E) Yourself

(F) Picture of the last person in your cell phone photos

The voice of the Lord should be part of your routine Christian lifestyle. You can hear God and minister to your family, coworkers, neighbors, whoever is around you. Don't limit the gift to only function in you for personal ministry to someone else. You can get a word for your job, your business— ask God what His thoughts are about things you're involved in. This invites God into whatever you're doing. You can prophecy, and you should prophecy. The word of the Lord is in your mouth—and if you don't release it, who will?

If you like these prophetic activations and desire to grow more in your prophetic gifting, we provide training twice a year, every January and September at Christian International. Rebecca and I are also available to bring our training sessions to churches and ministries to teach and activate the congregation or group.

ABOUT THE AUTHORS

Jermaine and Rebecca speak worldwide teaching and activating believers to hear God's voice. Jermaine is the author of *Break Up with Defeat*. Rebecca created a course helping first-time authors write Holy-Spirit inspired books that build the Kingdom of God. She is also the author of *Thx! The Secret to Being Grateful*. They are staff members at Christian International under the leadership of Dr. Bill Hamon.

Contact Information

INSTAGRAM

Jermaine-@kingjermaine

Rebecca-@RebeccajFrancis

FACEBOOK

www.facebook.com/jermaineafrancis

WEBSITE

JermaineandRebecca.com